Everybody's Guide to
SMALL CLAIMS COURT

California Edition

by RALPH WARNER
Research: David W. Brown

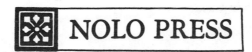 NOLO PRESS

950 PARKER STREET, BERKELEY, CA 94710

Printing History

Nolo Press is committed to keeping its books up-to-date. Each new printing, whether or not it is called a new edition, has been completely revised to reflect latest law changes. If you are using this book any considerable time after the last date listed below, be particularly careful not to rely on information without checking it.

First Edition	April 1978
Second Edition	February 1979
	July 1979
Third Edition	March 1981

Editor:	Leslie Ihara Armistead
Illustrations:	Linda Allison
Graphics:	Toni Ihara
Production:	Keija Kimura

Library of Congress Catalog No. 81-80355
ISBN 0-917316-35-5

THANK YOU

Nolo Press is as much family as business. Without the help of family members Trudy Ahlstrom, Toni Ihara, Keija Kimura, Linda Allison, Yolanda Gonzalez and Joel Shefflin, there would be no books such as this one.

A number of talented friends read the manuscript of this book and made helpful suggestions for improvement. With enough help, even a tarnished penny can be made to shine. Thanks to Dan Armistead, Leslie Ihara Armistead, Peter Honigsberg and Eileen Baris Luboff.

Special thanks to Ellen Roddy of the Small Claims Court Clerk's Office in Berkeley, California, who patiently answered hundreds of questions during the months that I was putting this book together and then made dozens of excellent suggestions for change after reading the manuscript. Thanks too, to Roger Dickinson of the State of California Department of Consumer Affairs, who doesn't always agree with what I write, but is, nonetheless, unfailingly helpful.

David Brown compiled the research for all material appearing in the Appendix. His thorough, patient and dedicated work have made this a better book. Here at Nolo Press we call him the research wizard.

CAUTION

CONTENTS

INTRODUCTION

Here is a practical book on how to use Small Claims Court. It is a tool which will help you answer such questions as:

"How does Small Claims Court work?"

"Do I have a case worth pursuing or defending?"

"How do I prepare my case to maximum advantage?"

"What witnesses and other evidence should I present?"

"What do I say in court?"

"Can I appeal if I lose?"

"How do I collect my judgment?"

Proper preparation and presentation of your Small Claims action can often mean the difference between receiving a check and writing one. This isn't to say that I can tell you how to take a hopeless case and turn it into a blue ribbon winner. It does mean that with the information you will learn here and your own creativity and common sense, you will be able to develop your position in the best possible way. It does mean that I can show you how a case with a slight limp can be improved and set on four good legs.

Just as important as knowing when and how to bring your Small Claims Court action is knowing when not to. You don't want to waste time and energy dragging a hopeless case to court. Here we will teach you to understand the difference between winners and losers, and hopefully to keep the losers at home.

The goal of this book is to give both people bringing a case and those defending one all the step-by-step information necessary to make the best possible use of Small Claims Court. From deciding whether you have a case, through gathering evidence, arranging for witnesses, planning your courtroom presentation, and collecting your money, you will find everything you need here.

Certain arbitrary decisions have had to be made as to order and depth of coverage. For example, the question of whether an oral contract is valid is discussed in Chapter 2, but not again in Chapter 16 on automobile repairs, where you may need it. So please take the time to read, or at least skim, the entire book before you focus on the chapters that interest you most. You may find something on page 106 that will change what you learned on page 32. A good way to get an overview of the entire Small Claims process is by carefully reading the Table of Contents. It would be worthwhile to read it through several times before starting the text itself.

Chapter 23 is the last part of this book designed to help you win your case and collect your money. Chapter 25 is devoted to a different cause — how our court system must be changed to deliver more justice and less frustration. In many ways this material is intensely personal in that it reflects my own experience with our formal, lawyer-dominated legal delivery system. It springs from my own painful realization that neither law, nor justice, nor the resolution of disputes is what our courts are presently about. We have instead allowed them to become the private fiefdom of lawyers, judges and other professionals, and it is their selfish interests rather than the common good that are being served.

I have included this material because I believe that it will be of interest to all of you who have become involved in the resolution of your own disputes in Small Claims Court. You have had the courage to take responsibility for solving your own problems. Given the opportunity, you can do a great deal more. It is past time that you are allowed to participate in your own legal system. It is past time that you are made welcome in your own courthouses. It is past time that all of us realize that a society whose legal system is run by and for lawyers can't long survive.

1

IN THE BEGINNING

A. FIRST THINGS

In this book we will be discussing Small Claims Court in California. As Small Claims procedures are established by state law, there are differences in their operating rules, state-to-state. Differences include such things as the maximum amount that you can sue for, who can sue, and what papers must be filed, where and when. However, the differences between Small Claims Court in California and other states tend to be those of detail, not substance. The basic approaches necessary to properly prepare and present a case are remarkably similar everywhere. For this reason, we have been able to also produce a 50 state version of this book. So, if you are outside of California, you will want to see *Everybody's Guide to Small Claims Court* (good in all 50 states) published by the Addison-Wesley Publishing Co. of Reading, Mass.

The purpose of Small Claims Court is to hear disputes involving small amounts of money, without long delays and formal rules of evidence. Disputes are presented by the people involved and lawyers are normally prohibited.* The maximum amount of

---

* In California, a lawyer may sue in his own case and as the representative of a corporation under some circumstances (see Chapter 8).

money that can be sued for in California is $750 (this is often called the "jurisdictional amount" in legal jargon). This is about average, although there is considerable variation with some states allowing Small Claims cases involving thousands of dollars, and others limiting Small Claims Court to cases worth no more than two or three hundred dollars.

In recent years the maximum amount for which suits can be brought has been on the rise and there are now proposals in the California legislature to raise it further. So don't rely on your memory, or what a friend tells you, or even what you read here. Call the local Small Claims Court clerk and find out exactly how much you can sue for. You may be pleasantly surprised and find that the maximum is more than you thought.

There are three great advantages of Small Claims Court. First, you get to prepare and present your own case without having to pay a lawyer more than your claim is worth.* This right to self-representation should be radically expanded to types of cases not now permitted in Small Claims Court. Unfortunately, such expansion runs counter to the self-interest of lawyers, who, like the czars of old Russia or the French nobility at the time of the Revolution, will fight to the death rather than ease the way for sensible reform.

The second great advantage to bringing a dispute to Small Claims Court is simplicity. The gobbledygook of complicated legal forms and language are kept to a minimum. To start your case, you need only fill out a few lines on a simple form (i.e., "Honest Al's Used Chariots owes me $500 because the 1972 Chevette they sold me in supposedly 'excellent condition' died less than a mile from the car lot."). When you get to court, you can talk to the judge without a whole lot of "res ipsa loquiturs" and "pendente lites". If you have documents, or witnesses, you may present them for what they are worth with no requirement that you comply with the thousand year's accumulation of fusty, musty procedures, habits and so-called rules of evidence of which the legal profession is so proud.

Third, and perhaps most important, Small Claims Court doesn't take long. Most disputes are heard in court within a month or two from the time the complaint is filed. The judge makes his (her) decision on the basis of what is presented in the courtroom, and

---

* People who have language difficulties are entitled to help in presenting their cases. Small Claims Court clerks maintain lists of volunteer interpreters.

normally renders a decision within a few days.

But before you decide that Small Claims Court sounds like just the place to bring your case, you will want to answer a basic question. Are the results you are likely to achieve in proportion to, or greater than, the effort you will have to expend? This must be answered individually, and the answers may be very different. It is all too easy to get so involved in a dispute that you lose sight of the fact that the time, trouble and expense of continuing are way out of balance with any likely return.

In order to profitably think about whether your case is worth the effort, you will want to understand the details of how Small Claims Court works — who can sue, where, for how much, etc. You will also want to learn a little law — are you entitled to relief, how much, and how do you compute the exact amount? Finally and most importantly comes the detail that so many people overlook to their later dismay. Assuming that you prepare and present your case brilliantly, and get a judgment for everything you request, can you collect? This seems a silly thing to overlook, doesn't it? Sad to say, however, it is often done. Plaintiffs commonly go through the entire Small Claims procedure with no chance of collecting a dime because they have sued a person with no money.

The purpose of the first dozen chapters of this book is to help you decide whether or not you have a case worth pursuing. These are not the Perry Mason sections where grand strategies are brilliantly unrolled to baffle and confound the opposition — that comes later. Here we are more concerned with what Della Street does off camera — such mundane tasks as locating the person you want to sue, suing in the right court, filling out the various forms and getting them properly served. Perhaps it will disappoint those of you with a dramatic turn of mind, but most cases are won or lost before anyone enters the courtroom.

Throughout this book we reproduce sample forms used in one or another judicial district in California. All California Small Claims contain about the same information although they are often laid out differently from one judicial district to the next. So, if you live in Los Angeles, don't be put off because we reproduce a San Francisco form, as the one in use in Los Angeles will be substantially similar. Blank copies of all these forms are available at your local Small Claims clerk's office. Forms in use outside of

California will look somewhat different, but you will find that they are easy to understand everywhere.

B. CHECKLIST OF THINGS TO THINK OUT BEFORE INITIATING OR DEFENDING YOUR CASE

Here is a sort of preliminary checklist of things you will want to think about at this initial stage. As you read further, we will go to each of these areas in more detail. But let me remind you again, if you haven't already gotten a copy of your local Small Claims Court rules, do it now. It's silly to come to bat with two out in the ninth and the bases loaded and not know if you are supposed to run to first or third.

Checklist of Questions Needing Answers Before You File in Small Claims Court:

1. Does the other person owe you the money, or, put another way, "is there liability"? (See Chapter 2)

2. How many dollars is your claim for? If it is for more than the Small Claims maximum, do you wish to waive the excess and still use Small Claims? (See Chapter 4)

3. Is your suit brought within the proper time period (Statute of Limitations)? (See Chapter 5)

4. What Small Claims Court should you bring your suit in? (See Chapter 9)

5. Whom do you sue? As you will see in many cases, especially those involving businesses and automobiles, this can be a little more technical and tricky than you might have guessed. (See Chapter 8)

6. Have you made a reasonable effort to contact the other party to offer a compromise? (See Chapter 6)

7. And again, the most important question —assuming that you can win, is there a reasonable chance that you can collect? (See Chapters 3 and 23)

Checklist of Questions Needing Answers Before Defending A Case:

1. Do you have a good defense to the claim of the plaintiff? (See Chapters 2 and 12)

2. Has the plaintiff sued for a reasonable or an excessive amount? (See Chapter 4)

3. Has the plaintiff brought his/her suit within the proper time limits (Statute of Limitations)? (See Chapter 5)

4. Has the plaintiff followed reasonably correct procedures in bringing suit and serving you with the court papers? (See Chapters , 11, 12)

5. Have you made a reasonable effort to contact the plaintiff in order to arrive at a compromise settlement? (See Chapters 6 and 12)

DEFENDANT'S NOTE: In addition to your right to defend a case, you also have the right to file your own claim (Chapters 10 and 12). You would want to do this if you believed that you suffered damage arising from the same incident or transaction that formed the basis of the plaintiff's suit against you, and that the plaintiff was responsible for your loss. Defendants' claims commonly develop out of a situation where both parties were negligent (say in a car accident) and the question to be decided is who was most at fault.

C. LEGAL JARGON DEFINED

Mercifully, there is not a great deal of technical language in use in Small Claims Courts. But there are a few times that may be new to you and which you will have to become familiar with. Don't try to learn all of these terms now. Refer back to these definitions when you need them.

ABSTRACT OF JUDGMENT: An official document which you get from the Small Claims Court clerk's office which shows you that you have a money judgment against another person.

CALIFORNIA CIVIL CODE (C.C.) and CALIFORNIA CODE OF CIVIL PROCEDURE (C.C.P.): Books which contain some of California's substantive and procedural laws. Available at all public libraries and law libraries which are located at the county courthouse and are open to the public.

CLAIM OF DEFENDANT: A claim by a defendant that the plaintiff owes him money. A Claim of Defendant is filed as part of the same lawsuit that the plaintiff has started.

CLAIM OF EXEMPTION: A procedure by which a "judgment debtor" can claim that under federal and/or California law certain of his money or other property is exempt from being grabbed to satisfy the debt.

CONTINUANCE: A court order that a hearing be postponed to a later date.

DEFAULT JUDGMENT: A court decision given when one person fails to show up (defaults).

DEFENDANT: The person being sued.

EQUITY: That amount of a particular piece of property that you actually own. For example, if a car has a fair market value of $2,000 and you owe a bank $1,000 on it, your equity is $1,000.

GARNISH: To attach money, usually wages or commissions, for payment of a debt.

HOMESTEAD DECLARATION: A piece of paper that any homeowner can file with the County Recorder's office which protects the equity in his/her home from attachment and sale to satisfy most debts. The protection is $45,000 in equity for a family and persons who are over 65 or blind, and $30,000 for a single person.

JUDGMENT: The decision rendered by the court.

JUDGMENT CREDITOR: A person to whom money is owed under a court decision.

JUDGMENT DEBTOR: A person who owes money under a court decision.

LEVY: A legal method to seize property or money for unpaid debts. For example, a sheriff could levy on (sell) your automobile if you refused to pay a judgment.

LIEN: A legal right to an interest in the property of another for payment of a debt. To get a lien you first must get a court judgment and then take proper steps to have the court enter an "Abstract of Judgment". You can then take the Abstract to the County Recorder's office in a county where the judent debtor has real property to establish the lien.

ORDER OF EXAMINATION: A court procedure allowing a creditor to question a debtor about the extent and location of his or her assets.

PLAINTIFF: The person who starts a lawsuit.

RECORDER (OFFICE OF THE COUNTY RECORDER): The person employed by the county to make and record documents. The County Recorder's office is usually located in the main county courthouse.

STATUTE OF LIMITATIONS: The time period in which you must file your lawsuit. It is normally figured from the date the act or omission giving rise to the lawsuit occurs and varies depending on the type of suit. See Chapter 5.

WRIT OF EXECUTION: An order by a court to the sheriff of a specific county to collect a specific amount of money due.

2

DO YOU HAVE A CASE?

Before you even start thinking about going to court — any court — you must answer a basic question. Do I have a good case?

Many mornings I have sat in Small Claims Court and watched people competently and carefully present hopeless cases. Why hopeless? Usually because the plaintiffs overlooked one of the most basic facts of litigation. Before you can collect for a loss you have suffered, you must show that the other party caused you to suffer the loss. Put into legal slang, this means that you must show that there is "liability". Obvious, you say. Perhaps it is to you, but apparently not to lots of others.

Here is what often seems to happen. People focus on their own loss — the amount of money that they are out as a result of whatever incident occurred. They think that, because they have been damaged, they must have a right of recovery against someone. But the fact that a loss has occurred isn't enough to make a winning case. You must also prove that the person you are suing is legally responsible to compensate you for the loss. Often doing this is easy and obvious and sometimes it is neither.

How do you establish that another person owes you money? Or put another way, how do you establish "liability"? Normally, you must establish at least one of the following three things. There are a number of technical legal defenses to all of these approaches, but for now, let's just look at the general theories.

1. That a valid contract (written, oral or implied) has been broken by the person you are suing and that, as a result, you have suffered money damages (see A below);

2. That the intentional behavior of the person you are suing has caused you to suffer money damages (see B below);

3. That the negligent behavior of the person you are suing has caused you to suffer money damages (see B below).

Before we look at each of these theories of "liability" in detail, let me tell you the story of a case I watched recently in Small Claims Court in Berkeley, California. The plaintiff (remember, the plaintiff is the person who initiates the lawsuit), a college student, had rented a parking space in the basement garage of an apartment house owned by defendant. There was a driveway entrance door to the garage that could be shut and locked, sealing the garage from the street. However, as the tenants were unwilling to go to the trouble of opening and closing the door, it always stood open. Indeed, the door had been open night and day for years, including the six months during which plaintiff had kept her car in the garage. There was also access to the garage from inside the building which contained 15 apartments, most of them occupied by more than one person.

One night someone entered the garage, smashed a window in plaintiff's (let's call her Sue) car and stole a fancy AM-FM radio and tape deck worth $528.50. Upon discovery of the theft, Sue immediately got several witnesses to the fact that her car had been broken into. She took pictures and then called the police. After the police investigation was complete, Sue obtained a copy of their investigation report. She also got several estimates as to the cost of repairing the damage to the car window, the lowest of which was $157.00. Sue then filed suit against the building owner for $685.50.

Sue overlooked only one thing. Unfortunately for her, it was an important one. Under the circumatances the building owner wasn't liable. He had never promised (orally or in writing) to keep the garage locked, had never done so, had never led Sue to believe that he would do so, and indeed could point to requests from other tenants that the garage be kept open. All the tenants were reasonably on notice that it was easy to gain access to the garage either from inside or outside the building. Put simply, the building owner was neither in violation of a contract, nor guilty of any negligent behavior in failing to lock the garage. The situation facing Sue was no different than it would have been if her car had been damaged in the street.

Now let's take this same situation, but change a few facts. Instead of a situation where the door was always open and no one ever expected it to be closed, let's now assume that the lease contract signed by the landlord and tenant stated that the tenant would be assigned a parking place in a "locked garage". Let's also assume that the garage had always been locked until the lock broke seven days before the theft occurred. Finally, let's assume that Sue and other tenants had asked the owner to fix the lock the day after it broke, but that he hadn't "gotten around to it".

In this situation, Sue should win. The landlord made certain promises to the tenant (to keep the garage locked) and then failed to keep them in a situation where he had ample opportunity to do so. The failure presumably allowed the robber access to the car.

NOTE: In both fact situations above, the total amount of damage $685.50, was the same. But in the first, there was not right of recovery (the defendant wasn't liable), and in the second, the apartment owner's failure to keep the door locked violated defendant's lease contract. In addition, the failure of the apartment owner to fix the lock within a reasonable time constituted negligence.

A. HOW TO APPROACH A BREACH OF CONTRACT CASE

In broad outline, a contract is any agreement between parties where one person agrees to do something for the other in exchange for something in return. The agreement may be written, oral, or implied from the circumstances (i.e., I deliver milk to your house and you pay for it).*

---

* Contracts that can't be performed within a year must be in writing. However, the great majority of consumer type contracts can be performed in a year and therefore oral contracts are normally enforceable.

EXAMPLE I: "I promise to give you $750 on the first of January ." This is not a contract because you have promised to do nothing for me in return. I have only indicated that I will give you a gift in the future. This sort of promise is not enforceable.

EXAMPLE II: "I promise to pay you $750 on January 1 in exchange for your promise to shine my door knob every morning before 7 o'clock." This is a valid contract. If I refuse to pay you, you can go to court and get a judgment for the $750.

Perhaps the largest number of cases coming before Small Claims Court involves the breach of a contract. Often the contract that has not been honored involves a failure to pay money. Hardly a day goes by when someone isn't sued for failing to pay the phone company, the milkman, the local hospital, or even book fines to the public library. But sometimes a breach of contract suit stems, not from failure to pay a bill, but because one party has performed his/her duties under the contract badly, or not at all, and the other person has been damaged as a result. Such might be the case if an apartment owner accepted a deposit and agreed to rent an apartment to a tenant and then rented it to someone else.*

Damages resulting from a breach of contract are normally not difficult to prove. You must show that the contract existed (if it is written, it should be presented to the court, and if it's oral or implied from the circumstances, it should be stated). You must then testify as to the circumstances of the other person's breach of the contract and the amount of damages you have suffered. In many situations this involves no more than stating that a legitimate bill for X dollars has not been paid.

EXAMPLE: "Joe Williams owes me $200 because he failed to pay for car repairs that he asked me to perform. I did all the repairs properly. Here is a work order signed by Joe authorizing me to do the work."

The fact that many contract cases are easy to win doesn't mean that all are. I have seen a good number of plaintiffs lose what to them seemed open and shut cases. Why? Simply because they failed to show that defendant owed them any money. Put another way: they failed to show that a contract existed (Example II below). In other situations the plaintiff is able to show that a

---

* Leases and rental agreements, whether written or oral, are contracts. They are discussed in detail in the *California Tenants' Handbook* (Fifth Edition), Nolo Press (see back of this book).

contract existed, but not that defendant breached it (Example I below).

EXAMPLE I: Let's go over the facts of a situation that I witnessed recently in Small Claims Court in Oakland, California. Plaintiff sued defendant for $350, the cost of replacing a pigskin suede jacket that was ruined by defendant's cleaning establishment. Plaintiff had taken the jacket to defendant for cleaning and given him a $25 fee. Defendant, by accepting the jacket and the fee, clearly implied that he would properly clean the jacket. A contract existed.

Plaintiff was very sure of his loss. He stood in the courtroom, a great bear of a man, looking as if he had just escaped from a professional football team and slowly put the jacket on. As he wiggled into the coat, the whole courtroom, including the judge who almost choked trying to keep a straight face, burst out laughing. With a little luck the jacket would have fit a good-sized jockey. The sleeves barely came to the man's elbows and the coat itself didn't reach his waist.

As I sat watching, I thought that the case was over and that the plaintiff had won easily. Certainly by putting on the jacket he had made his point more effectively than he could have with ten minutes of testimony. I was wrong. The plaintiff had overlooked two things, one obvious, and one not so obvious. The defendant, a clever man, started his testimony and by the time he was done, the plaintiff's case had shrunk almost as much as the jacket.

The obvious thing that plaintiff overlooked in asking for the $350 replacement value of the jacket was that the jacket was two years old and had been worn a good bit. Valuation is a common problem in clothing cases and we discuss it in detail in Chapters 4 and 21. Let's just say here that the jacket was worth no more than $200 in its used condition and that, in any case where your property is damaged or destroyed, the amount of your recovery will be limited to the fair market value of the goods at the time the damage occurs — not their replacement value.

Now let's look at defendant's other defense. He testified that, when he saw the jacket after cleaning, he had been amazed. His cleaning shop specialized in leather goods and the process used should have resulted in no such shrinking problem. What's more, he testified that he had examined a number of other goods in the same cleaning batch and found no shrinking problem with any of them. To find out what happened , he sent the jacket to an "independent testing laboratory". Their report, which he presented to the court, stated that the problem was not in the cleaning, but in the jacket. It was poorly made in that the leather had been severely overstretched prior to assembly . When it had been placed in the cleaning fluid, it had shrunk as a result of this poor original workmanship.

What happened? The judge was convinced by the testing lab report and felt that defendant had breached no contract as far as the cleaning was concerned.* However, he also felt that defendant, as a leather cleaning specialist, had a responsibility to notify plaintiff that the jacket should not have been cleaned in the first place. Therefore, the judge held mostly for the defendant, but did award the plaintiff $50 in damages.

EXAMPLE II: A few weeks later I saw another contract case where the plaintiff had suffered an obvious loss, but failed to show that defendant was responsible for making it good. This time it was a plaintiff landlord suing the parent of a tenant for damages that the tenant had done to her apartment. The parent was sued because he had co-signed his daughter's lease contract. The plaintiff easily convinced the judge that the damage had, in fact, occurred and the judge seemed disposed toward giving judgment for the $580 requested until the parent presented his defense. He showed that the lease between his daughter and the landlord had been rewritten three times after he originally co-signed the agreement without his again adding his signature. He claimed that, because he had not co-signed any of the subsequent lease contracts, he wasn't liable. The judge agreed. The judge was probably relying on the noteworthy case of *Wexler v. McLucas,* 48 CA3 Supp 9 (1975). Leases, rental agreements and the rights and responsibilities of co-signers are discussed in more detail in the *California Tenants' Handbook,* Moskovitz, Warner and Sherman, Nolo Press.

NOTE: We will get into individual fact situations of contracts more in Chapters 16-21. Before you decide whether or not you have a good case, read on.

---

* Plaintiff could still bring suit against the person who made the jacket for defective workmanship. It could be argued that, by using inferior material, they had breached an implied warranty (contract) that the goods sold were reasonably fit.

B. HOW TO APPROACH A CASE WHERE YOUR PROPERTY HAS BEEN DAMAGED BY THE NEGLIGENT OR INTENTIONAL ACTS OF SOMEONE ELSE

After cases involving breach of contract, the most common disputes that come to Small Claims Court involve damage to one person's property caused by the negligent actions of another. Less often, the plaintiff claims that he suffered loss because the defendant intended to damage his belongings.

A technical definition of what constitutes negligence could easily fill the next few pages. Indeed, whole law texts have been written on the subject. I remember thinking in law school that the more the scholarly professors wrote the more mixed up they got. Like good taste or bad wine, negligence seems to be easy to recognize, but hard to define.

Here is a one sentence definition. If, as a result of another person's conduct, your property is injured and that person didn't act with reasonable care in the circumstances, you have a case based on his negligence.* It's as simple — or complex — as that. If you want to get into the gory details of the subject, go to your nearest law library and get any recent text on "Torts". "Torts" are wrongful acts or injuries.

EXAMPLE: Jake knows the brakes on his ancient Saab are in serious need of repair, but does nothing about it. One night when the car is parked on a hill, the brakes fail and the car rolls across the sidewalk and destroys Carolyn's pomegranate tree. Carolyn sues Jake for $125.00, which is the reasonable value of the tree. Jake would lose because he did not act with reasonable care in the circumstances.

Another obvious situation involving negligence would be the car or bus that swerves into your driving lane and sideswipes your fender. The driver of the offending vehicle had a duty to operate it in such a way as to not harm you, and failed to do so. A situation where negligence could be difficult to show might involve your neighbor's tree that falls on a car parked in your driveway. Here you have to be ready to prove that for some reason (age, disease, an obviously bad root system, etc.) the tree was in a weakened condition, and the neighbor was negligent in failing to do something about it. If the tree had looked to be in good health, you would have a tough time proving that your neighbor was negligent in not cutting it down or propping it up.

There is no fool-proof way to determine in advance if someone is or is not negligent. It's often a close question — a matter of judgment. If you are in doubt, bring your case and let the judge decide. After all, he or she gets paid (by you) to do it.

---

* Sometimes negligence can occur when a person who has a duty or responsibility to act fails to do so. For example, a car mechanic who fails to check your brakes after promising to do so would be negligent.

Here are a couple of questions which may help you make a decision as to whether you have a good case based on someone else's negligence.*

★ Did the person whose act (or failure to act) injured you behave in a reasonable way? Or to put it another way, would you have behaved differently if you were in his or her shoes?

★ Was your conduct partly the cause of the injury?

If you believe that the person who caused you to suffer a monetary loss behaved in an unreasonable way (ran a red light when drunk) and that you were acting sensibly (driving at 30 m.p.h. in the proper lane), you probably have a good case. If you were a little at fault (slightly negligent), but the other fellow was much more at fault (very negligent), you can still recover in California and most other states. If a judge finds that one person (drunk and speeding) was 80% at fault and that the other (slightly inattentive) was 20% at fault, the comparatively innocent party can recover 60% of his or her loss.

C. HOW TO APPROACH A PERSONAL INJURY CASE

The considerations here are much the same as outlined in the section B just above. You must show not only that you were injured but that someone's intentional or negligent behavior caused your injury.*

EXAMPLE I: Keija takes Harry, her Pekinese puppy, for a walk without a leash. Soto walks by and Harry takes an instant dislike to his purple and orange socks and shows it with a quick nip on Soto's right ankle. As Soto was on a public sidewalk where he had a right to be, we can safely assume that Keija was negligent in allowing Harry to bite him. Why? Because, as a society, we have decided that you can't let your dog run about biting people in public places, even if they do have horrible taste in socks. If you do, you are negligent and are going to have to pay for it.

EXAMPLE II: Now, let's change our example and assume that, instead of biting Soto, Harry went after a burglar who was trying to sneak into Keija's garage window. Let's also assume that after

---

* There is also a concept called "strict liability". This concept is applied to such things as nuclear reactors, munitions storage, people who keep wild and inherently dangerous animals (a cheetah in the city) and other extremely hazardous activities. Anyone injured by an inherently hazardous activity can recover without showing either negligence or intent to harm. This is because, when a high level of danger is present, the person undertaking the activity is "strictly liable" for any and all injuries.

the dust cleared and the cops hauled the burglar away it was discovered that he had suffered the same injury as Soto. Although the burglar's blood was just as red as Soto's, he can recover nothing. Why? Because Keija is entitled to protect herself and her property and as a society we have decided that keeping a dog with sharp teeth is a reasonable way to do it.

Now let's change the example again. This time Harry bites Walter, Keija's next door neighbor, who had climbed over the back yard fence to get some apples from Keija's tree. Keija knew that the neighbor took the apple, but never encouraged him to do so. The neighbor knew that Harry was in the yard and that Harry's slogan seemed to be "if it moves, bite it". Here again, there would be no liability. Keija had taken reasonable precautions to secure Harry in her own yard. She owed no duty of care to her apple-poaching neighbor in this situation.

I know you're getting sick of hearing about nasty little Harry, but bear with him a moment longer. Let's assume now that Harry bites a travelling carrot-peeler salesman who knocks at the front door. Can the salesperson recover? Probably. Even though Keija didn't invite him and never let a carrot in the house, the salesperson had the right to assume that it was safe to go up the walk to the front door. But suppose Keija had a fence around the front yard with a latched gate and a "Beware of the Dog" sign, complete with a picture of Harry hanging onto someone's leg? This would be enough to satisfy Keija's duty of care to the rest of the world and if the carrot-peeler salesman entered the gate anyway, he would do so at his own risk.

SUGGESTION: Before you sue someone for a personal injury (or for property damage), think about whether they owed you a duty of care and whether they breached that duty. If in doubt, go ahead and sue, but be prepared to deal with this question ("liability") as well as simply showing the extent of your injury. In later chapters I will give you some practical advice as to how to prove your case.

D. STATING YOUR CLAIM ON YOUR COURT PAPERS

Before you get too far into theories of law, let me bring you back to earth for a minute. While it is helpful to have a good grasp on what's involved in proving a contract or negligence case (the judge, after all, is a lawyer), it is also essential that you stay grounded on the facts of your grievance. One of the joys of Small Claims Court is that you don't plead theories of law — you state facts.

Let's jump ahead and take a look at the form you will fill out when you file your case. Turn to Chapter 10 and find the form entitled "Plaintiff's Statement". Look at Line 5. As you can see, there is little space for theory. Indeed, there is barely room to set down the facts of your dispute. You should state your case like this:

"I took my coat to John's Dry Cleaners and it was returned in a damaged (shrunk) condition."

"Defendant's dog bit me on the corner of Rose and Peach Streets in West Covina, California."

"The car repairs that Joe's Garage did on my car were done wrong, resulting in my engine burning."

"Defendant refused to return the cleaning deposit for my apartment even though I left it clean."

NOTE: When you state your case on the court papers, your only goal is to notify the other party and the court as to the broad outlines of your dispute. You don't want to try to argue the facts of your case or the law that you believe applies to it. Your chance to do this will come later in court.

IMPORTANT: Now is a good time to start organizing your materials in one place. Get a couple of manila envelopes or file folders, label them carefully, and find a safe place for storage. One folder or envelope should be used to store all documentary evidence such as receipts, letters, photographs, etc. The other is for your court papers, filing fee receipts, etc. It's no secret that more than one case has been won or lost because of good (or bad) record keeping.

3

CAN YOU RECOVER IF YOU WIN?

This is the shortest chapter in the book and the most important. In it, I ask all of you who are thinking of filing a Small Claims suit to focus on a very simple question — can you collect if you win? Collecting from many individuals or businesses isn't a problem as they are solvent and will routinely pay any judgments entered against them. But all too often, the main problem you face in Small Claims Court is not winning your case, but collecting your money when you do win.

I am co-author with Peter Jan Honigsberg of the book published by Nolo Press entitled *The California Debtors' Handbook – Billpayers' Rights*. It contains information for people who are over their heads in legal debts and don't know how they are going to keep the roof over their heads and clothes on their kids' backs. The message of the book is that, surprisingly, there are many ways for a debtor to protect himself. A creditor can't take the food from the debtor's table, or the T.V. from his living room, or even the car from his driveway.*

---

* A debtor's car is protected only if he has $500 or less equity in it, unless he uses the car as a tool of his trade, in which case the car is exempt from attachment as long as the equity is $2,500 or less. C.C.P. 690.4, 690.2.

What do these facts mean to you? Simply that many Californians who are not completely without money are nevertheless "judgment proof". You can sue them and get judgments against them until red cows dance on the yellow moon, but you can't collect a dime. Unfortunately, just this sort of frustrating thing happens every day — people go to lots of trouble to win cases only to realize that the judgment is uncollectable. This, of course, compounds the misery. Not only has the person suing lost the money from the original debt or injury, but also the time, trouble and expense of the Small Claims suit. As my grandmother used to say, "no one ever got to live in the big house on the hill by throwing a good quarter after a bad dime."

Whenever a dispute develops, it is all too easy to get caught up in thinking and arguing about who wronged them. So easily , that perspective is lost and the problems of collection are forgotten. I emphasize this because I have so often observed people bringing cases to court in which there was never a hope of collecting. How can I tell ahead of time? I can't always, but in many situations, it's not hard. One thing I look for is whether or not the defendant is working. If a person fails to voluntarily pay a judgment, the easiest way to collect it is to garnish his or her wages. Thus, if the person sued is working, there is an excellent chance of collecting if payment is not made voluntarily. But you can't garnish a welfare, social security, unemployment, pension or disability check. So, if the person sued gets his income from one of these sources, red flags are flying.

But what about other assets? Can't a judgment be collected from sources other than wages? Yes, it can — bank accounts, motor vehicles and real estate are other common collection sources. But did you know that while you can levy on a checking account, or other account in a state or federally chartered bank, savings accounts up to $1,000 in a savings and loan association are exempt? Did you know that you can't effectively get at the equity in a family house unless it exceeds $45,000, or that a whole list of other possessions including furniture, a car with $500 or less in equity, the tools of a person's trade, or $1,500 in a credit union are exempt?* So before you go down and file your papers, ask

---

* Each state has a list of "exempt" property. Check your state's statutes. In California property that is exempt from being taken to satisfy debts is listed in Code of Civil Procedure Section 690. Also, see the *California Debtors' Handbook - Bill Payers' Rights,* Warner and Honigsberg, Nolo Press, $6.95 (order information at back of this book). The *Debtors' Handbook* contains forms and instructions necessary for a debtor to take advantage of his/her rights.

yourself these questions:

1. Does the person you wish to sue voluntarily pay debts — or are you dealing with a person who will make it as difficult as possible to collect if you win?

2. Does he/she have a job?

3. If this person doesn't have a job, does he or she have some other means of support or assets that convince you that you can collect?

4. If you have your doubt about voluntary payment and the person you are suing doesn't have a job, can you identify some non-exempt assets that you can attach, such as a bank account, or real property other than the place where the person lives?

5. If a business is involved, is it solvent and does it have a good reputation for paying debts?

NOTE: If a person or a business declares bankruptcy and lists you as a creditor, your right to recover is cut off. If you are owed money on a secured debt (there was a security agreement as in the case of a car or major appliance), you are entitled to recover your security.

In Chapter 23, we deal in detail with the mechanics of collecting after you get your judgment. If you think that this may pose a problem, you will wish to read this chapter now. But remember what my canny, old grandmother said about bad dimes and good quarters and don't waste your time chasing people who have no money.

4

HOW MUCH CAN YOU SUE FOR?

The maximum amount you can sue for in Small Claims Court varies from state to state. In California it is $750.* As I suggested in Chapter 1, if you are not in California, you should get the rules that affect you by calling your local Small Claims Court clerk. With minor exceptions Small Claims Court does not hear cases unless they are for money damages. This means that you can't use Small Claims Court to get a divorce, stop (enjoin) the city from cutting down your favorite oak tree, change your name, or do any of the thousands of other things that require some solution other than the payment of money. In California, Small Claims Court can also be used for certain types of evictions (see Chapter 20) and in rare situations, equitable relief (see Section D of this chapter).

Just because you have a claim which is less than the Small Claims maximum doesn't mean that you must sue in Small Claims Court. You can sue in Municipal (or Justice) Court on a $50 claim if you wish, but if you do, you must follow all their formal rules and pay filing fees that will average $25–$50. Unfortunately, this role is often abused by businesses which file small cases in Municipal Court because it is harder for the non-lawyer to respond in a

---

* This is the limit for 1981. There is some hope that it will be raised for 1982.

34

situation where formal pleadings are required. Accordingly, we favor legislation to require that all cases that can be brought in Small Claims Court be brought in that court.

Why is Small Claims Court limited to such small amounts and to cases involving money? Well, the traditional assumption has been that people aren't very competent to deal with their own legal affairs. Only lawyers, it was thought, were clever enough to handle anything but the most inconsequential claims. Who made these assumptions? We all have, but we have been encouraged to do so by lawyers themselves, who have long dominated our state legislatures where our court rules are made. Somehow, as a society, we have allowed lawyers to metamorphose from dry, little men in English villages with little more going for them than an ability to read and write and a fire-proof box in which to store papers, to self-proclaimed superpeople who seem convinced they have been given a mandate to run the world. Small Claims Courts have been tolerated in part as a direct result of this growth in lawyers' egos. Lawyers have become so important in their own eyes that it is somehow beneath their dignity to become involved in disputes over piddling amounts.

But times are starting to change. All sorts of people are beginning to realize that our legal system is staggering under a heavy load of favoritism, waste and archaic and often nonsensical rules designed primarily by and for lawyers. One result of this realization is a growing interest in expanding Small Claims Courts. In some states Small Claims Court jurisdiction has already been substantially increased. As you might guess, lawyers regard this expansion much as they would a 500 pound bear stepping slowly on their toes.

California, with its Small Claims maximum of $750, is about average.* If you are in a state where the amount is higher or lower, simply substitute your amount whenever you read $750 here. Knowing the largest amount for which you can sue is important, but it is only one of many facts that you will have to deal with in deciding how much you wish to demand when you fill out your papers. Here are some other things to think about.

A. CUTTING DOWN A CLAIM THAT'S OVER THE LIMIT TO FIT IT INTO SMALL CLAIMS COURT

It is legal to reduce an excessive claim so that it will fit into Small Claims Court. Thus, you could take a $1,350 debt and bring it into Small Claims Court, claiming only $750. But if you do this, you forever waive the $600 difference between $750 and $1,350. In

---

* Costs, such as filing fees, serving of process, fees where witnesses are subpoenaed, etc., are recoverable in addition to the $750 maximum.

legal parlance, this is called "waiving the excess". Why wouldn't this be a silly thing to do? It would be if it wasn't for the insanity of our court system where the alternative to Small Claims Court involves filing your suit in a formal court with dozens of complicated rules and the considerable expense involved in having a lawyer draw up papers, etc. A lawyer would probably charge considerably more than $600 to represent you. It is possible to represent yourself in Municipal or Superior Court, but doing so requires a good bit of homework and the guts to walk into an unfamiliar and sometimes hostile arena.* I don't mean to discourage you. Lots of people have successfully handled their cases in our formal courts, but you should be aware before you start that your path may be lonely and frustrating. If you wish to take your case to Municipal or Superior Court yourself, you might start by looking at a series of books entitled *California Forms*. This encyclopedia-like series shows you how to prepare most of the papers that you will ever need to file.

B. SPLITTING SMALL CLAIMS COURT CASES

It is not legal to split an over-the-limit claim into two or more pieces to fit each into Small Claims Court. Taking the $1,350 figure we used above, this means that you couldn't sue the same person separately for $700 and $650.** As with most rules, however, a little creative thought will take you a long way. While you can't split a case that's too big to get it into Small Claims Court, you can bring multiple suits against the same person as long as they are based on different claims. This is where the creativity comes in. There is often a large grey area in which it is genuinely difficult to differentiate between one divided claim and several independent ones. If you can reasonably argue that a $1,350 case actually involves two or more separate contracts, or injuries to your person or property, you may as well try dividing it. The worst that will happen is that a judge will disagree and tell you to make a choice between taking the entire claim to Municipal Court, or waiving any claim for money in excess of $750 and staying in Small Claims.

---

* Law libraries exist in most major courthouses and are open to the public. Law librarians are usually very helpful in assisting you to find materials.

** Defendant's claims that are over the $750 limit are discussed in Chapters 10 and 12.

EXAMPLE 1: Recently I watched a man in the private telephone business come into Small Claims Court with three separate lawsuits against the same defendant for a combined total of $2,000. One, he said, was for failure to pay for phone installation, another was for failure to pay for phone maintenance and the third was for failure to pay for moving several phones to a different location. The man claimed that each suit was based on the breach of a separate contract. The judge, after asking a few questions, told the man that he was on the borderline between one divided (no good) and several separate (O.K.) claims, but decided to give him the benefit of the doubt and allowed him to present each case. The man won all three and got two judgments for $700 and a third for $600.

EXAMPLE 2: Another morning a woman alleged that she had lent a business acquaintance $750 twice and was therefore bringing two separate suits, each for $750. The defendant said that this wasn't true. She claimed that she had borrowed $1,500 on two installments. A different judge, after listening to each person briefly, told the plaintiff that only one claim was involved and that, if she didn't want to waive all money over $750, she should go to Municipal Court.

SUGGESTION: If you wish to sue someone on two related claims, which you believe can be viewed as being separate, you may be better off to file your actions a few days apart. This will result in their being heard on different days, and in most metropolitan areas, by different judges. Unless the defendant shows up and argues that you have split one claim, you will likely get your judgments without difficulty. There is, however, one possible drawback to this approach. If you bring your claims in on the same day and the judge rules that they are one claim, he will give you a choice as to whether to waive the excess over $750 or go to Municipal Court. However, if you go to court on different days and the question of split claims is raised on the second or third day, you may have a problem. If the judge decides that your action in splitting the claims was improper, he has no choice but to throw the second and third claims out of court with no opportunity to refile in Municipal Court. This is because you have already sued and won and you are not entitled to sue the same person twice for the same claim.

C. HOW TO COMPUTE THE EXACT AMOUNT OF YOUR CLAIM

Sometimes it's easy to understand exactly what dollar amount to sue for, but often it's tricky. Before we get to the tricky part, let's go over the basic rule. When in doubt, always bring your suit a little on the high side. Why? Because the court has the power to award you less than you request, but can't give you more, even if the judge feels that you are entitled to it. But don't go overboard — if you sue for $750 on a $100 claim, you are likely to spur your opponent to furious opposition, ruin any chance for an out-of-court compromise, and lose the respect of the judge.

1. Computing The Exact Amount — Contract Cases

To arrive at the exact figure to sue on in contract cases, compute the difference between the amount you were supposed to receive under the contract and what you actually received. For example, if Jeannie Goodday agrees to pay Homer Brightspot $1200 to paint her house to look like a rainbow, but then only gives him $800, Homer has a claim for $500 plus the cost of filing suit and serving Jeannie with the papers (costs are discussed in more detail in Chapter 15). The fact that Jeannie and Homer made their agreement orally does not bar Homer from suing. Oral contracts are OK as long as they can be carried out in a year. Of course, people tend to remember oral contracts differently and this can lead to serious proof problems once you get to court. It is always wise to reduce agreements to writing, even if only to a note or letter agreement dated and signed by both parties.

Where the contract involves lending money in exchange for interest, don't forget to include the interest due in the amount you sue for.* I have seen several disappointed people sue for the exact amount of the debt (say $500) and not include interest (say $50), thinking that they could have the judge add the interest when they got to court. This can't be done — the judge doesn't have the power to make an award larger than the amount you request. Of course, you can't sue for interest if the interest amount would make your claim larger than the Small Claims maximum.

---

* As a general rule you can only recover interest when it is called for in a written or oral contract. If you loaned a friend $100, but never mentioned interest, you can sue only for the return of the $100.

Unfortunately, not all claims based on breach of contract are easy to reduce to a money amount. This is often due to a legal doctrine known as "mitigation of damages". Don't let the fancy term throw you. Like so much of our law the concept behind the "mumbo jumbo" is simple. "Mitigation of damages" means simply that the person bringing suit for breach of contract must himself take all reasonable steps to limit the amount of damages he suffers. Let's take an example from the landlord-tenant field. Tillie the tenant moves out three months before the end of her lease (remember a lease is a contract). Her monthly rent is $250. Can Lothar the landlord recover the full $750 ($250 x 3 months) from Tillie in Small Claims Court? Probably not. Why? Because Lothar has control of the empty apartment and must take reasonable steps to attempt to find a new tenant. If Lothar can re-rent the apartment to someone else for $250 or more per month, he has suffered no damage. Put another way, if Lothar re-rents the apartment, he has fulfilled his responsibility to "mitigate damages". In a typical situation it might take Lothar several weeks (unless he had plenty of advance notice, or Tillie herself found a new tenant) to find a suitable new tenant. If it took three weeks and $25 worth of newspaper ads, Lothar could recover approximately $200 from Tillie.

The "mitigation of damages" concept isn't only applicable to landlord-tenant situations, but applies to every contract case where the person damaged can take reasonable steps to protect himself or herself. In the earlier example, if Jeannie Goodday had agreed to pay Homer Brightspot $100 per day for seven days to paint her house and then had cancelled after the first day, Homer could sue her for the remaining $600, but, if he did, he would surely be asked whether he had earned any other money during the six days. If he had, it would be subtracted from the $600. But what if Homer refused other work and slept in his hammock all week? If Jeannie could show that he had turned down other jobs, or had refused to make reasonable efforts to seek available work, this too would be used to reduce Homer's recovery.

SUGGESTION: Sue only for the amount of money you are out. Don't try to collect money in court that you have already recovered from someone else.

2. Computing The Exact Amount — Property Damage Cases

When your property has been damaged by the negligent or intentional act of someone else, you have a right to recover for your loss.* This amount is often, but not always, the amount of money that it would take to fix the damaged item.

EXAMPLE: John Quickstop bashes into Melissa Caretaker's new Dodge, smashing in the left rear. How much can Melissa recover? The amount that it would cost to fix, or, if necessary, replace the damaged part of her car. Melissa should get several estimates from responsible body and fender shops and sue for the amount of the lowest one, if John won't pay voluntarily (see Chapter 19).

There is, however, a big exception to the rule that a person who has had property damaged can recover the cost of fixing the damaged item. This occurs when the cost to fix the item exceeds its actual cash market value. You are not entitled to a new or better object — only to have your loss made good. Had Melissa Caretaker been driving a 1961 Dodge, the cost to fix the fender might well have exceeded the value of the car. If this were the case, she would be entitled to the value of the car, not the value of the fender repair.

Think of it this way. In any situation where the value of the repair exceeds the value of the object, you are limited to the fair market value of the object (what you could have sold it for) a

---

* If you haven't already done so, read Chapter 2. It is important to remember that you not only have to establish the amount of your damage, but that the person you are suing is legally responsible ("liable") to pay your damages.

minute before the damage occurred. From this figure, you have to subtract the value, if any, of the object after the injury. Of course, in deciding how much to claim, you should give yourself the benefit of the doubt as to how much a piece of property is worth, but don't be ridiculous. A $300 motor scooter might conceivably be worth $450 or $500 but it's not worth $750.

EXAMPLE: Let's return to Melissa. If her 1961 Dodge was worth $700 and the fender would cost $800 to replace, she would be limited to a $700 recovery, less what the car could be sold for in its damaged state. If this was $50 for scrap, she would be entitled to $650. However, if Melissa had just gotten a new engine and transmission and her car was worth $1,200, she would legally be entitled to recover and sue for the entire $800 needed to get her Dodge fixed. To sue in Small Claims Court, however, she would have to reduce her claim to the $750 court maximum.

NOTE: Many people insist on believing that they can recover the cost of getting a replacement object when theirs has been totalled. As you should now understand, this isn't necessarily true. If Melissa's $700 car was totalled and she claimed that she simply couldn't get another decent car for less than $900, she would still be limited to recovering $700. To get $900 she would have to show that her car had a sale value of that much just before the accident. This rule can cause you a real hardship when an older object that is in great shape is destroyed. The fair market value may be low, while the cost of replacement high.

Knowing what something is worth and proving it are quite different. A car that you are sure is worth $800 may look like it's only worth $500 to someone else. In court you will want to be prepared to show that your piece of property is worth every bit of the $800. Perhaps the best way to do this is to get some estimates (opinions) from experts in the field (i.e., a car dealer if your car was ruined). This is best done by having the expert come to court and testify, but can also be done in writing. You will also want to check newspaper and flea market ads for the prices asked for comparable goods and creatively explore any other approaches that make sense given the type of damage you have suffered. We talk more about proving your case in court in Chapters 16-21.

3. Computing The Exact Amount — Cases Involving Damage To Clothing

Clothing is property so why am I separating it out for special treatment? For two reasons. Cases involving clothing are extremely common in Small Claims Court and judges seem to apply a logic to them that they apply to no other property damage cases. The reason for this is that clothing is personal to its owner and often has small or little value to anyone else even though it may be in good condition. If the rules that we just learned (i.e., you can recover the repair cost of a damaged item unless this would be more than its market value before the damage occurred, in which case you are limited to recovering its total value) were strictly applied to clothing, there would often be little or no recovery. This is because there is not much market for used clothing.

When suing for damage to new or almost new clothing, sue for its cost. If it is older, sue for that percentage of the value of the clothing which reflects how worn it was when the damage occurred. For example, if your two year old suit which cost $400 new were destroyed, sue for $200 if you feel the suit would have lasted another two years. In clothing cases most judges want answers to these questions: How much did the clothing cost originally? How much of its useful life was consumed at the time the damage occurred? Does the damaged item still have some value to the owner, or has it been ruined?

EXAMPLE 1: Wendy took her new $250 coat to Rudolph, a tailor, to have alterations made. Rudolph cut part of the back of the coat in the wrong place and ruined it. How much should Wendy sue for? $250 as the coat was almost new. She could probably expect to recover close to this amount.

EXAMPLE 2: The same facts as just above but the coat was two years old and had been well worn. Here Wendy would be wise to sue for $200 and hope to recover $150.

EXAMPLE 3: Again Wendy and the coat. This time we will return it to its almost new condition, but have Rudolph slightly deface the back, instead of completely destroying it. I would still advise Wendy to sue for the full $250. Whether she could recover that much would depend on the judge. Most would probably award her a little less on the theory that the coat retained some value. Were I Wendy, however, I would strongly argue that I didn't buy the coat with the expectation that I could only wear it in a closet and that, as far as I was concerned, the coat was ruined. (See

Chapter 21 for more detail if you are arguing a clothing case in Small Claims Court.)

4. Computing The Exact Amount — Personal Injury Cases

Lawyers quickly take over the great majority of cases where someone is injured. These claims are routinely inflated (a sprained back might be worth $3,000-$5,000 or more), because it is in everyone's selfish interest to do so. The insurance adjusters and insurance company lawyers are as much a part of this something-for-nothing syndrome, as are the ambulance-chasing plaintiff's attorneys. If there aren't lots of claims, lots of lawsuits, lots of depositions and negotiations, it wouldn't take lots of people making lots of money to run the system. Even in states with co-called "no-fault" automobile insurance, the dispute resolution bureaucracy has managed to protect itself very well.

Some small personal injury cases do get to Small Claims Court, however. Dog bite cases are one common example and there are others. Here is how you figure the amount to sue for:

Out of pocket medical costs,
including medical transportation   _____

Loss of pay, or vacation time
for missing work   _____

*Pain and suffering**   _____

TOTAL **   _____

Medical and hospital bills including transportation to and from the doctor are routinely recoverable as long as you have established that the person you are suing is at fault. However, if you are covered by health insurance and the insurance company has already paid your medical costs, you will find that your policy says that any money that you recover for these costs must be turned

* In more serious cases you would also have to figure the monetary value of any permanent injury. These cases do not, however, get to Small Claims Court.
** Often a personal injury is accompanied by injury to property. Thus, a dog bite might also ruin your pants. You add all of your damages together as part of the same suit. You can't sue separately for your pants and your behind.

over to the company. Often, insurance companies don't make much effort to keep track of, or recover, Small Claims judgments as the amounts of money involved don't make it worthwhile. Knowing this, many judges are reluctant to grant judgments for medical bills unless the individual can show that they are personally out-of-pocket the money.

Loss of pay or vacation time is viewed in a similar way. If the cocker spaniel down the block lies in wait for you behind a hedge and grabs a piece of your derriere for breakfast, and as a result you miss a day of work getting yourself patched up, you are entitled to recover the loss of any pay, commissions or vacation time. However, if you are on a job with unlimited paid sick time, so that you suffer no loss for missing work, you have nothing to recover.

The third area of recovery is for what is euphemistically known as "pain and suffering". This is a catch-all phrase that simultaneously means a great deal and nothing at all. Generations of lawyers have made a good living mumbling it. Their idea is often to take a minor injury (sprained ankle) and inflate its value as much as possible by claiming that the injured party underwent great "pain and suffering". "How much is every single minute that my poor client suffered an unbearably painful ankle worth — $1.00, $5.00, $10,000?" etc. When you read about million dollar settlements, a good chunk of the recover routinely falls in the "pain and suffering" category. I don't mean to suggest that recovery for "pain and suffering" is always wrong — just that it is often abused.

But back to the case of the nasty cocker spaniel. If you received a painful bite, spent the morning getting your rump attended to, had to take several pain killers and then make sure that the dog was free of rabies, you would very likely feel that you were entitled to some recovery. One judge I know doesn't pay much attention to the evidence in this type of case. He simply awards $250 for a bite by a medium-sized dog, adds $100 for anything the size of a lion, and subtracts $100 if the dog looks like a mouse.

SUGGESTION: In thinking about how much you wish to sue for, be aware that lawyers often bring suit for three to four times the amount of the out-of-pocket damages (medical bills and loss of work). Therefore, if you were out of pocket $150, you might wish to ask for $500, the overage being for "pain and suffering". If you have no medical bills (there is no blood, or at least x-rays), you will find it difficult to recover anything for "pain and suffering". This is why lawyers routinely encourage their clients to get as much medical attention as possible. Or as my friend Anne-Therese says, "The squeaky wheel gets the grease".

EXAMPLE 1: Mary Tendertummy is drinking a bottle of pop when a mouse foot floats to the surface. She is greatly nauseated, loses her lunch and goes to the doctor for medication. As a result, she loses an afternoon's pay. She sues the pop company for $500. This is reasonable. She will probably recover most of this amount.

EXAMPLE 2: The same thing happens to Roy Toughguy. He just throws the pop away in disgust and goes back to work. A few weeks later he hears about Mary's recovery and decides that he too could use $500. How much is he likely to recover? Probably not much more than the price of the soda — he apparently suffered little or no injury.

NOTE: Certain costs of suit such as filing fees, subpoenaed witness fees, costs of serving papers, etc., can be recovered, but many, such as compensation for time off from work to go to court, transportation to and from court, etc., cannot. See Chapter 15 for more information. You do not add costs to the amount of your suit. The judge does this when the case is decided.

D.   EQUITABLE RELIEF (OR MONEY CAN'T ALWAYS SOLVE THE PROBLEM)

Nearly half the states, including California, allow judges to grant relief (providing you ask for it) in ways that do not involve the payment of money, if equity (fairness) demands it. In California (Code of Civil Procedure Section 116.3), "equitable relief" is limited to one or more of four categories: "recission," "restitution," "reformation," and "specific performance." Let's translate these into English.

RECISSION: This is a remedy that is used when a grossly unfair or fraudulent contract is discovered or where a contract was based on a mistake as to an important fact. Thus, if a merchant sued you for failure to pay for aluminum siding that you contended had been misrepresented and was a total rip-off, you could ask that the contract be rescinded.

RESTITUTION: This is an important remedy. It gives a judge the power to order that a particular piece of property be transferred to its original owner when fairness requires that the contracting parties be restored to their original positions. It could be used in the common situation in which one person sells another a piece of property (say a motor scooter) and the other fails to pay. Instead of simply giving the seller a money judgment which might be hard to collect, the judge now has the power to order the scooter restored to its original owner.

REFORMATION: This remedy is somewhat unusual. It has to do with changing (reforming) a contract to meet the original intent of the parties in a situation where some term or condition agreed to by the parties has been left out and where fairness dictates that this be done. Thus, if Arthur the Author and Peter the Publisher orally agree that Peter will publish Arthur's 200-page book and then they write a contract inadvertently leaving out the number of pages, a court would very likely "reform" the contract to include this provision if Arthur showed up with a 750-page manuscript. Reformation is most commonly used when an oral agreement is written down wrong.

SPECIFIC PERFORMANCE: This is an important remedy that comes into play where a contract involving an unusual or "one-of-a-kind" object has not been carried out. Say you agree to buy a unique antique jade ring for your mother's birthday that is exactly like one she lost years before, and then the seller refuses to go through with the deal. A court could cite the doctrine of "specific performance" to order that the ring be turned over to you. "Specific performance" will only be ordered in situations where the payment of money will not make a party to a contract whole.

NOTE: In filling out your court papers you will still be required to indicate that the value of the item for which you want equitable relief is under the Small Claims maximum. Thus, you might describe the nature of your claim (Chapter 10, Step 1) as follows: "I want the delivery of a 'one-of-a-kind' antique jade ring worth approximately $700 according to my contract with defendant."

Oops! It's sometimes difficult to get court clerks to understand what you mean when you ask for equitable relief — indeed, most that we have talked to haven't developed any forms to handle these claims and quite a few had never even heard of the possibility of a Small Claims Court judge being able to grant "equitable relief." So, if you run into reactions that border on disbelief when you ask if equitable relief remedies are possible, refer the clerk (and maybe even the judge) to Section 116.3 of the Code of Civil Procedure and remind the judge that he or she does have the power to grant equitable relief.

5

IS THE SUIT BROUGHT WITHIN THE PROPER TIME LIMITS (STATUTE OF LIMITATIONS)?

Each state sets up time limits within which lawsuits must be filed. These are called Statutes of Limitations. Time limits are different for different types of cases. If you wait too long, your right to sue will be barred by these statutes. Why have a Statute of Limitations? Because it has been found that disputes are best settled soon after they develop. Unlike wine, lawsuits don't improve with age. Memories fade and witnesses die or move away, and once-clear details tend to blur together. As a general rule, it is wise to sue as soon after your dispute arises as is reasonably possible. Statutes of Limitations are almost never less than one year, so if you file promptly, you should have little to worry about.

A. CALIFORNIA STATUTE OF LIMITATIONS PERIODS*

PERSONAL INJURY: One year from the injury, or, if the injury was not immediately discovered, one year from the date it was discovered.

---

* I only include the most common Statutes of Limitations periods here. You will find the rest in California C.C.P. Sections 312-363.

ORAL CONTRACTS: Two years from the day the contract was broken.

WRITTEN CONTRACTS: Four years from the date of breach of contract.

DAMAGE TO PERSONAL OR REAL PROPERTY: Three years from the date the damage occurs.

FRAUD: Three years from the date of the discovery of the fraud.

SUITS AGAINST PUBLIC AGENCIES: Before you can sue a city, county or the state government, you must file an administrative claim form. The time period in which this must be done is normally 100 days. This is not precisely a Statute of Limitations, but it has the same effect. (See Chapter 8 for a more complete discussion of how to sue governments in Small Claims Court.)

NOTE: Some contracts which you may assume to be oral may actually be written. People often forget that they signed papers when they first arrange for goods or services. For example, your charge accounts, telephone service, insurance policies as well as most major purchases of goods and services involve a written contract, even though you haven't signed any papers for years. And another thing — to have a written contract you need not have signed a document full of "whereas's" and therefores. Any signed writing can be a contract even if it's written on toilet paper with lipstick. When you go to a car repair shop and they make out a work order and you sign it — that's a contract. (See Chapter 2 for more about contracts).

If you live outside of California, you will wish to check your state's Statute of Limitations Periods if any considerable time has passed between the time an incident occurred and the time you file suit. You will find a set of your state's laws at a public library or a law library which you will find located at the local courthouse. Check the index under "Statute of Limitations" or just "Limitations". If you have trouble finding what you need, ask the librarian for help. Librarians positively enjoy finding things.

B. COMPUTING THE STATUTE OF LIMITATIONS

O.K., now let's assume that you have found out what the relevant limitations period is. How do you know what date to start your counting from? That's easy. Start with the day the injury to your person or property occurred, or, if a contract is involved, start with the day that the failure to perform under the terms of the contract occurred. Where a contract to pay in installments is involved, start with the day that the first payment was missed.

EXAMPLE: Doolittle owes Crabapple $500, payable in five monthly installments of $100. Both live in San Jose, California. They never wrote down any of the terms of their agreement. Doolittle misses his third monthly payment which was due on January 1, 1979. Crabapple should compute his Statute of Limitations period from January 2, 1979 assuming, of course, that Doolittle doesn't later catch up on his payments. Since the Statute of Limitations period for oral contracts is two years, this means that Crabapple has until January 1, 1981 to file his suit. If a written contract had been involved, Crabapple could file until January 1, 1983, as the Statute of Limitations on written contracts is four years.

I am frequently asked to explain the legal implications of the following situation. After the Statute of Limitations runs out (say two years on an oral contract to pay for having a fence painted), the debtor commences voluntarily to make payments. Does the voluntary payment have the effect of creating a new two year Statute of Limitations period, allowing the person who is owed the money to sue if the debtor again stops paying? In most states including California, simply starting to pay on an obligation barred by the Statute of Limitations doesn't create a new period for suit.* All the creditor can do is to keep his toes crossed and hope that the debtor's belated streak of honesty continues. However, if the debtor signs a written agreement to make the payments, this does create a new Statute of Limitations period. In legal slang this is called "reaffirming a debt".

EXAMPLE: Back to the drama of Doolittle and Crabapple. Let's assume that in February, 1981, Doolittle experiences a burst of energy, gets a job and decides to pay off all of his old debts. He sends Crabapple $50. A week later, suffering terrible strain from getting up before noon, he quits his job and reverts to his old ways of sleeping in the sun when not reading the racing form. Is

---

* See California Code of Civil Procedure Section 360.

the Statute of Limitations allowing Crabapple to sue reinstated? No. As we learned above, once the limitation period of two years has run out, it can't be revived by simply making a payment. However, if Doolittle had sent Crabapple the $50 and had also included a letter saying that he would pay the remainder of the debt, Crabapple would again be able to sue and get a judgment if he failed to pay. Why? Because a written promise to pay a debt barred by the Statute of Limitations has the legal effect of re-establishing the debt.

C. TELLING THE JUDGE THAT THE STATUTE OF LIMITATIONS HAS RUN OUT

What should a defendant do if he believes that the Statute of Limitations period has run out? Tell the judge. Sometimes a judge will figure this out without a reminder, but sometimes he won't. If you are a defendant, don't ever assume that because the clerk has filed the papers and you have been properly served, this means that the plaintiff has started his or her suit on time. The clerk never gets involved in Statute of Limitations questions. They will cheerfully file a suit brought on a breach of contract occurring in 1916.

6

HOW TO SETTLE YOUR DISPUTE

Litigation should be a last, not a first, resort. Suing is not as bad as shooting, but neither is it as much fun as a good back rub. Rarely does anyone have a high time in court. In addition to being time-consuming and emotionally draining, lawsuits tend to polarize disagreements into all win-all lose propositions where face (and pocketbook) saving compromise is difficult. Most of us are terrified of making fools of ourselves in front of strangers. When forced to defend our actions in a public forum, we tend rather regularly to adopt a most self-righteous view of our own conduct, and to attribute the vilest of motives to our opponents. Many of us are willing to admit that we have been a bit of a fool in private — especially if the other person does too — but in public, we will stonewall all the way, even when it would be to our advantage to appear a little more fallible.

I have witnessed dozens of otherwise sensible people litigate the most appalling trivia including one case in which the parties effectively tied up over $2,000 of each other's property (and had a fist fight) over a fishing pole worth $15. This doesn't mean that I don't think you should pursue your case to court if necessary.

What I am suggesting is this: before you file your case, ask your-self whether you have done everything reasonably possible (and then a little more) to try to settle the case.

A. TRY TO TALK YOUR DISPUTE OUT

Making an attempt to settle your case isn't a waste of time. Indeed, you are required to make the attempt. The law in many states including California states that a "demand" for payment be made prior to filing a court action. Increasingly the "demand" requirement is being interpreted to mean that the "demand" be in the form of a letter.

But first things first. Before you reach for pen and paper, try to talk to the person with whom you are having the dispute. I can't count how many times clients have consulted me about sup-posedly insurmountable disputes in situations where they had never once tried to talk it out with the other person.* Apparently many of us have a strong psychological barrier to talking to peo-ple we are upset with, especially if we have already exchanged heated words. Sometimes we seem to think that a willingness to compromise shows weakness. But wasn't it Winston Churchill who said, "I would rather jaw, jaw, jaw than war, war, war"?

IMPORTANT: An offer of compromise made either orally or in writing, does not bind the person making the offer to that amount if the compromise is not accepted. Thus, you could make an original demand for $500, then offer to compromise for $350, and, if your compromise offer was turned down, still sue for $500.

If you take my advice and again try to talk things out with your opponent and are successful, write down your agreement. Oral understandings, especially between people who have small con-fidence in one another, are often not worth the breath used to speak them out. Here are two sample compromise forms that you may be able to adopt to your uses.

---

* Just before making final revisions on this chapter, I sat as judge pro tem in a case where one man sued another for $500 resulting from a car accident. The defendant "was willing to pay", he said. "Why haven't you paid before?" I asked. "No one asked me to," he replied.

Dusty Rider and Bigshot Owner agree as follows:

1. Dusty was to exercise Bigshot's horses every morning for two weeks from October 1 to October 15 at Golden Gate Fields Racetrack in Albany, California, and was to be paid $15 per horse exercised each morning;

2. Bigshot's horses got sick on September 29 and there was no need for Dusty's services;

3. Dusty gave up other employment to make herself available to ride Bigshot's horses, and she couldn't find another riding job at short notice;

4. Dusty and Bigshot agree that $600 is fair compensation for her loss of work and Dusty agrees to accept this amount as a complete settlement of all of her claims.

Date	Dusty Rider
Date	Bigshot Owner

Walter Spottedhound and Nellie Neighbor agree that Walter's "mixed breed" black dog Clem sneaked onto Nellie's patio and bit her behind the right knee. After taking into consideration Nellie's medical bills, the fact that she had to miss two hours' work while at the doctor's office, and the pain and discomfort she has suffered, it is agreed that Walter will pay her $250 in full settlement of all her claims. The money will be paid in five equal monthly installments. The first installment is hereby paid this date and the next four will be paid on the first day of February, March, April and May 1978.

It is also agreed that Walter will commence at once to construct a fence to keep Clem out of Nellie's yard.

Date	Walter Spottedhound
Date	Nellie Neighbor

B. WRITE A "DEMAND" LETTER

If your efforts to talk your problems out fail (or despite my urging you refuse to try), your next step is to send your adversary a letter. As noted above, many courts require that a "demand" letter be sent. But even if there is no such requirement, it is almost essential that you send one. Why? Simple — the "demand" letter is not only useful in trying to settle your case, it is your best opportunity to lay your case before the judge in a carefully organized way. In a sense, it allows you to manufacture evidence that you will be permitted to use in court if the case isn't settled. Either way, you can't lose, so take the time to write a good letter.

Your letter should be reasonably short, directly to the point, and, above all, polite (you catch more flies with honey than by hitting them over the head with a mallet). Use a typewriter and keep a carbon, or photocopy. Limit your remarks to a page, or at most, a page and a half. Remember, if the case doesn't settle, you will want to show the letter to the judge — and what's more important, you will want the judge to read it. It's my experience that aside from letters of the heart, no one ever reads much more than a page with anything like attention.

Remember, the judge doesn't know anything about how your problem started and developed. This means that you will want to write the letter so that it briefly reviews the entire dispute. It may seem a little odd, writing all the facts for your opponent who well knows them, and it may result in a formal sounding letter. So what? You want to produce a result that the judge can understand.

Let's consider a case I watched in Los Angeles the other morning. The facts (with a little editorial license) were simple. Jennifer moved into Peter's house in August, agreeing to pay $150 per month rent. The house had four bedrooms, each occupied by one person. The kitchen and other common areas were shared. Things went well enough until one chilly evening in October when Jennifer turned on the heat. Peter was right behind her to turn it off, explaining that heat inflamed his allergies.

As the days passed and fall deepened, heat became more and more of an issue until one cold, late November night when Jennifer returned home from her waitress job to find her room "about the same temperature as the inside of an icicle". After a short cry, she started packing and moved out the next morning. She refused to pay Peter any additional rent, claiming that she was within her rights to terminate her month-to-month tenancy without giving notice because the house was uninhabitable.* It

---

* In California, tenants do have the right to simply leave, or in the alternative, to stay and cease paying rent if conditions in their rented home become uninhabitable whether the cause is no heat, water, electricity, etc. See the *California Tenants' Handbook*, Moskovitz, Warner and Sherman, Nolo Press (order information at back of the book).

took Peter one month to find a suitable tenant and to have that person move in. Therefore, he was without a tenant for one month and lost rent in the amount of $150.

After calling Jennifer several times and asking her to make good the $150 only to have her slam down the phone in disgust, Peter wrote her the following letter:

```
                                        61 Spring St.
                                        Los Angeles, Calif.

                                        January 1, 1979


Jennifer Tenant
111 Sacramento St.
Palos Verdes, Calif.

Dear Jennifer:

    You are a real idiot.  Actually you're worse than that: you're malici-
ous - walking out on me before Christmas and leaving me with no tenant
when you know that I needed the money to pay my child support.  You know
that I promised to get you an electric room heater.  Don't think I don't
know that the real reason you moved out was to live with your boyfriend.

    Please send me the $150 I lost because you didn't give me a month's
notice like the law says you are supposed to.  If you don't, I will sue
you.


                            In aggravation,


                            Peter Landperson
```

To which Jennifer replied:

```
                                        111 Sacramento St.
                                        Palos Verdes, Calif.

                                        January 4, 1979


Peter Landperson
61 Spring St.
Los Angeles, Calif.

Dear Mr. Landperson:

    You nearly froze me to death, you cheap bastard.  I am surprised it
only took a month to rent that iceberg of a room - you must have found
a rich polar bear (ha ha).  People like you should be locked up.

    I hope you choke on an ice cube.


                            Jennifer Tenant
```

57

As you no doubt have guessed, both Peter and Jennifer made similar mistakes. Instead of being business-like, each deliberately set out to annoy the other, reducing any possible chance of compromise. In addition, they each assumed that they were writing only to the other, forgetting about the judge. Thus, both lost a valuable chance to present the judge with a coherent summary of the facts as they saw them. As evidence in a subsequent court proceeding, both letters were worthless.

[Now let's interrupt these proceedings and give Peter and Jennifer another chance to write sensible letters.]

---

61 Spring St.
Los Angeles, Calif.

January 1, 1979

Jennifer Tenant
111 Sacramento St.
Palos Verdes, Calif.

Dear Jennifer:

As you will recall, you moved into my house at 61 Spring St., Los Angeles, California, on August 1, 1978, agreeing to pay me $150 per month rent on the first of each month. On November 29 you suddenly moved out, having given me no advance notice whatsoever.

I realize that you were unhappy about the fact that the house was a little on the cool side, but I don't believe that this was a serious problem as the temperature was at all times over 60^0 and I had agreed to get you an electric heater for your room by December.

I was unable to get a tenant to replace you (although I tried every way I could and asked you for help) until January 1, 1979. This means that I am short $150 rent for the room you occupied. If necessary, I will take this dispute to court because, as you know, I am on a very tight budget. I hope that this isn't necessary and that we can arrive at a sensible compromise. I have tried to call you with no success. Perhaps you can give me a call in the next week to talk this over.

Sincerely,

Peter Landperson

To which our now enlightened Jennifer promptly replied:

```
                                    111 Sacramento St.
                                    Palos Verdes, Calif.

                                    January 4, 1979


        Peter Landperson
        61 Spring St.
        Los Angeles, Calif.

        Dear Peter:

            I just received your letter concerning the rent at 61 Spring St. and
        am sorry to say that I don't agree either with the facts as you have pre-
        sented them, or with your demand for back rent.

            When I moved in August 1, 1978, you never told me that you had an al-
        lergy and that there would be a problem keeping the house at a normal
        temperature.  I would not have moved in had you informed me of this.

            From early October when we had the first cool evenings, all through
        November (almost 2 months), I asked that you provide heat.  You didn't.
        Finally it became unbearable to return from work in the middle of the
        night to a cold house which was often below 60°.  It is true that I
        moved out suddenly, but I felt that I was within my rights under Calif-
        ornia law which states that a tenant need not pay rent for an uninhab-
        itable space (see the California Tenants' Handbook, Moskovitz, Warner
        and Sherman).

            Since you mentioned the non-existent electric heater in your letter,
        let me respond to that.  You first promised to get the heater over a
        month before I moved out and never did.  Also, as I pointed out to you
        on several occasions, the heater was not a complete solution to the
        problem as it would have heated only my room and not the kitchen, liv-
        ing room, dining area, etc.  You repeatedly told me that it would be im-
        possible to heat these areas.

            Peter, I sincerely regret the fact that you feel wronged, but I be-
        lieve that I have been very fair with you.  I am sure that you would
        have been able to re-rent the room promptly if the house had been warm.
        I regret that I don't believe that any compromise is possible and that
        you will just have to go to court if that's what you wish to do.


                                    Sincerely,



                                    Jennifer Tenant
```

As you can see, while the second two letters are less fun to read, they are far more informative. Both Peter and Jennifer have clearly set forth their positions. The goal of reaching an acceptable compromise was not met, but both have prepared a good statement of their positions for the judge. Of course, in court, both Peter and Jennifer will testify, present witnesses, etc. in addition to their letters, but court proceedings are often rushed and confused and it's nice to have something for the judge to fall back on. Be sure to bring the carbon copy (xerox) of your demand letter to court when your case is to be heard. Be sure, too, that the judge is given the copy as part of your case. The judge won't be able to guess that you have it; you will have to let him or her know and hand it to the clerk. (For more about what happens in court, see Chapters 13-15.)

IMPORTANT: If you compromise your case after you have filed it in court, but before the court hearing, be sure to do so in writing. Also let the court know that you won't be appearing. Some courts will ask that the plaintiff sign a "Request for Dismissal" form. Never do this unless your compromise agreement has already been reduced to writing. Also, it is not wise to have a case dismissed unless you have been paid in full, as once the case is dismissed, you can't refile it. Thus, if the compromise settlement involves installment payments, it would be wise to go to court and present it to the judge. He or she can then enter a judgment in the same terms as the compromise. If this is done and then the judgment is not paid, it can be collected using the techniques discussed in Chapter 24.

C. SETTLEMENT AT COURT

Sometimes cases are settled in court while you are waiting for your case to be heard. It is perfectly proper to ask the other person if he or she wishes to step into the hall for a moment to talk the matter over. If you can agree on a compromise, wait until the case is called and tell the judge the amount you have agreed upon and whether the amount is to be paid all at once, or over time. The judge can either order the case dismissed if one person pays the other on the spot, or can enter a judgment for the amount that you have compromised upon, if payment is to be made later.

D. MEDIATION AS AN ALTERNATIVE

Here are Nolo Press we are enthusiastic about the recent trend away from the adversary approach to dispute resolution and toward efforts to help people solve their own disputes by talking them out with the help of a trained mediator. The idea is to get the parties to arrive at an agreement —usually a reasonable compromise —that seems fair to all. For more information on mediation, see *The People's Law Review,* which contains a lot of material on mediation and the many mediation projects around the United States (order information at the back of this book).

Unfortunately, at least as far as Small Claims Court is concerned, California lags behind In giving people the opportunity to mediate their disputes. Unlike New York City, for example, where everyone is offered an arbitration-mediation alternative to a court trial, mediation is currently available only in Santa Monica, with the help of the Neighborhood Justice Center in Venice—Mar Vista. In that city, litigants are given the voluntary opportunity to meet with a mediator as an alternative to the formal Small Claims procedure. Where mediation is attempted, it is successful as much as 80 per cent of the time.

7

WHO CAN SUE?

In most situations, asking who can sue in Small Claims Court is an easy question. You can as long as you are eighteen years of age, have not been declared mentally incompetent in a judicial proceeding and are suing on your own claim.* Sometimes, however, listing yourself as the party bringing suit isn't quite so easy.

Here are the rules:

1. If you are suing for yourself alone , simply list your full name where it says "Plaintiff" on the "Plaintiff's Statement" and sign the "declaration under penalty of perjury" on the "Claim of Plaintiff" form (see sample forms in Chapter 10).

2. If more than one person is bringing suit, list all the names on the "Plaintiff's Statement". Only one person need sign the "declaration under penalty of perjury" stating that all the information given is true and correct (see Chapter 10).

3. If you are filing a claim on behalf of an individually-owned business, the owner of the business must do the suing. He/she should list his/her name and the business name as plaintiffs on the "Plaintiff's Statement". The "declaration under penalty of perjury" should be signed in the business owner's name (see Chapter 10).

---

* Minors emancipated under Sections 60–70 of the California Civil Code can also sue and be sued. This includes minors on active duty with the military, married minors and minors emancipated by court order.

4. If you are filing a claim on behalf of a partnership, list the partnership name as plaintiff. Only one of the partners need sign the "declaration under penalty of perjury" (see Chapter 10).

5. If you are filing a claim on behalf of a corporation, whether profit or non-profit, list the corporation as plaintiff. The "declaration under penalty of perjury" must be signed by either:

   a) an officer of the corporation

         or

   b) a person authorized to file claims on behalf of the corporation by the Board of Directors of the corporation.

If a non-officer of a corporation is involved, the court clerk will want to see some documentation that the person suing is properly authorized. Here is a sample authorization statement that you can use. If you use a particular Small Claims Court regularly, you can often file a copy of the authorization in its permanent file.*

RESOLUTION - SMALL CLAIMS

APPOINTING A CORPORATION REPRESENTATIVE

It appears to the Board of Directors of ____Acme Illusions, Inc._____

_____.

a corporation, qualified to do business in the State of California, that it is necessary to appoint an agent for this corporation to act for and in its behalf in the Small Claims Court of ____Oakland-Piedmont_____Judicial District, County of _Alameda_____, State of California, that ____KEIJA SOTO_____ is a suitable individual for such appointment.

It is therefore resolved that ____KEIJA SOTO_____ be and ___he is appointed to represent and appear for said corporation in the lawful process of any and all claims filed in the above named court, and ___he is further authorized to accept service of process issued by said court, for and on behalf of said corporation.

I certify that foregoing resolution was adopted by the Board of Directors of this corporation, at a regular meeting of said board, held on ____(Date)_____ .

Tom Jake
Secretary

(SEAL)

The local business address of this corporation is: Acme Illusions, Inc.
100 Primrose Path
Oakland, CA

Keija Soto
(Signature of agent so appointed)

41 Mandrake, Oakland, CA.
(Address of agent)

---

* Local rules differ as to requirements for filing on behalf of a corporation. Some courts no longer require an authorization adopted by the Board of Directors. Call your Small Claims clerk.

6. When a claim arises out of damage to a motor vehicle, the registered owner(s) of the vehicle must file in Small Claims Court. This means that, if you are driving someone else's car and get hit by a third party, you can't sue for damage done to the car. The registered owner must do the suing.

7. If you are suing on behalf of a public entity such as a public library, city tax assessor's office or county hospital, you must show the court clerk proper authorization to sue.

A. PARTICIPATION BY ATTORNEYS

Attorneys, or other people acting as representatives, cannot normally appear in Small Claims Court. There are several exceptions to this rule. The major one allows attorneys to appear to sue or defend their own claims. Attorneys are also allowed to use Small Claims Court to sue or defend on behalf of a partnership when all other partners are also attorneys, and on behalf of a professional corporation of which the attorney is an officer or a director and all other officers and directors are attorneys (C.C.P. 117.4).

B. SUITS BY MINORS

If you are a minor (have not yet reached your eighteenth birthday), your parent or legal guardian must sue for you, unless you are emancipated under Sections 60–70 of the California Civil Code. To do this, a form must be filled out and signed by the judge appointing the person in question as your "Guardian Ad Litem." This simply means guardian for the purposes of the lawsuit. Ask the court clerk for a "Petition for Appointment of Guardian Ad Litem" form.

Here is a sample. It must be signed by both minor and guardian. When you have filled it out, take it to the Small Claims Court clerk and arrange to have the judge add his signature at the bottom, under "ORDER".

179-191

Space below for use of Court Clerk only

SMALL CLAIMS COURT FOR THE   JUDICIAL DISTRICT
        COUNTY OF ALAMEDA, STATE OF CALIFORNIA

. . . .
                                    PLAINTIFF S: No.   SC

            vs.
                                                        PETITION AND ORDER FOR
                                                        APPOINTMENT OF GUARDIAN AD LITEM

. . . . DEFENDANT(S)

ABBREVIATED TITLE:

PETITION

I, _____
                   (NAME OF MINOR, OR NAME AND STATUS OF PROPOSED GUARDIAN AND NAME OF MINOR)

a minor, of the age of _____ years and the _____ in the above entitled cause,
                                                       (PLAINTIFF DEFENDANT)

request that _____ be appointed guardian ad litem of the within named
              (NAME OF PROPOSED GUARDIAN)

minor.

Dated _____   _____
                                                        PETITIONER

CONSENT OF GUARDIAN

I consent to my appointment as guardian ad litem for _____
                                                                   (NAME OF MINOR)

in the above entitled cause and agree to serve in that capacity.

Dated _____   _____
                                                        GUARDIAN

ORDER

It is ordered that the above petition be granted and that _____
                                                                  (NAME OF GUARDIAN)

be appointed guardian ad litem for and on behalf of the above named minor in the above entitled cause.

Dated _____   _____
                                                  JUDGE OF THE MUNICIPAL COURT

                                                        C.C.P. 372, 373

It used to be that the owners of small unincorporated businesses were discouraged from using Small Claims Court. This was because there was a legal requirement that stated that the owner of the business had to file the papers himself or herself and show up in court. For example, a dentist who wished to sue on an overdue bill would have to be in court personally. But California and a number of other states are more understanding of business time pressures and allow both incorporated and unincorporated businesses to send employees to court when the case involves unpaid bills. Thus, in California it would be proper for the dentist (or dress maker) to send the person who keeps the books to court when a bill isn't paid (C.C.P. 117.4)*

NOTE: California forbids the use of Small Claims Court by "assignees" (a fancy term that usually refers to collection agencies).

---

* Remember, as I discuss earlier in this chapter, in California an incorporated business (whether profit or nonprofit) can appoint a representative to appear on its behalf in Small Claims Court for all types of claims.

8

WHO CAN BE SUED?

You can sue just about anybody (person, partnership, corporation, government, etc.) in Small Claims Court. Indeed, it is more often the "where can I sue" problem (see Chapter 9), not the "who can I sue" problem that causes difficulties. For example, you can sue David Rockefeller or the Chase Manhattan Bank, but you will find it very difficult to have the case heard in Sacramento, California or Emporia, Kansas, unless you can show that Rockefeller or the bank lives or does business there, or entered into or agreed to carry out a contract with you there. This doesn't mean that you have a problem with suing Rockefeller or the bank — you don't. The problem is only with suing in Sacramento or Emporia. If you go to New York where both Rockefeller and the bank are located, you can bring your suit with no problem.

Here are some hints that may prove helpful when it comes to filling out your papers. Again, the information I give here is based on California rules. You will want to check the forms set out in Chapter 10 B as you go along.

A. SUING ONE PERSON

If you are suing an individual, simply name him or her, using the most complete name that you have for that person. If the person calls himself J.R. Smith and you don't know what the J. stands for, simply sue him as J.R. Smith.

B. SUING TWO OR MORE PEOPLE

If you are suing more than one person on a claim arising from the same incident or contract, you must list and serve (see Chapter 11) each to properly bring them before the court. With a husband and wife, you must list each separately.

EXAMPLE: J.R. and June Smith, who are married, borrow $400 from you to start an avocado pit polishing business. Unfortunately, in the middle of the polishing, the seeds begin to sprout. J.R. and June get discouraged and refuse to pay you. If you wish to sue them and get a judgment, you should list them as J.R. Smith and June Smith — not Mr. and Mrs. Smith. But now suppose that J.R. borrowed $400 for the avocado pit business in January, June borrowed $500 to fix her motorcycle a month later and neither loan was repaid. In this situation, you would sue each in separate Small Claims actions.

C. SUING AN INDIVIDUALLY OWNED BUSINESS

Here you list the name of the owner and the name of the business (i.e., J.R. Smith — doing business as [d.b.a.] Smith's Texaco. Don't assume that the name of the business is in fact the same as the name of the owner. Often it is not. Jim's Garage may be owned by Pablo Garcia Motors, Inc. (see Section E below). If you get a judgment against Jim's Garage and there is no Jim, you will find that it's worthless, unless you take steps to have the judgment changed to reflect the correct name under C.C.P. Section 117.19. This can take time and trouble so be sure you know who the owner of the business is before you sue.

California requires that all people doing business in a name other than their own file a Fictitious Business Name Statement with the county clerk in the county or counties in which the business operates. This is public information and you can get it from the court clerk. Another way to figure out who owns a business is to check with the Business Tax and License Office in the city where the business is located. If the business is not in an incorporated area, try the county. The tax and license office will have a list of the owners of all businesses paying taxes in the city. They should be able to tell you, for example, that the Garden of Exotic Delights is owned by Rufus Clod. Once you find this out, you sue Rufus Clod, d.b.a. The Garden of Exotic Delights.

If for some reason the tax and license office and the county clerk can't help, you may want to check with the state. Millions of people, from exterminators to embalmers, must register with one or another office in Sacramento. So, if your beef is with a teacher, architect, smog control device installer, holder of a beer or wine license, etc., you will very likely be able to learn who and where they are with a letter or phone call. Check the Sacramento County phone book under California.

NOTE: If you do sue the owner of a business using a fictitious name under an incorrect name, C.C.P. Section 117.19 allows you to substitute the correct name either at the court hearing or after judgment. Ask the Small Claims Court clerk for more information.

D. SUING PARTNERSHIPS

List the names of all the business partners even if your dispute is only with one (Patricia Sun and Farah Moon, d.b.a. Sacramento Gardens). See Section C just above for information on how to learn just who owns what. Never assume that you know who owns a business without checking. All partners to a business are individually liable for all the acts of the business.

EXAMPLE: You go to a local cleaners with your new, sky blue suit. They put too much cleaning fluid on it with the result that a small grey cloud settles on the rear right shoulder. After unsuccessfully trying to get the cleaners to take responsibility for improving the weather on the back of your suit, you start thinking about a different kind of suit. When you start filling out your court papers (see Chapter 10), you realize that you know only that the store says "Perfection Cleaners" on the front, and that the guy who has been so unpleasant to you is named Bob. You call the city business tax and license people and they tell you that Perfection Cleaners is owned by Robert Johnson and Sal De Benno. You should sue both and also list the name of the business.

NOTE: It is wise to get a judgment against more than one person if possible. When it comes to trying to collect, it's always nice to have someone in reserve if one defendant turns out to be an artful dodger.

E. SUING A CORPORATION

Corporations are legal people. This means that you can sue, and enforce a judgment against, a corporation itself. You should not sue the owners of the corporation or its officers or managers as individuals unless you have a personal claim against them that is separate from their role as part of the corporation. In most situations the real people who own or operate the corporation aren't themselves liable to pay for the corporation's debts. This is called "limited liability" and is part of the reason that many people choose to incorporate.

Be sure to list the full name of the corporation when you file suit (John's Liquors, Inc., a Corporation). Here again, the name on the door or the stationery may not be the real name. Corporations too sometimes do business using fictitious names. Check with the city or county business license people where the corporation does business. In addition, the California Secretary of State's office, Corporate Status Unit, 111 Capitol Mall, Sacramento, California 95814 maintains a complete list of all California corporations, and all out-of-state corporations "qualified" to do business in California.

F. SUING ON A MOTOR VEHICLE ACCIDENT

Here there are some special rules. If your claim arises from an accident with an automobile, motorcycle, truck or R.V., you must name both the driver of the vehicle and the registered owner as part of your suit. Most times you will have gotten this information at the time of the accident. If a police accident report was made, it will also contain this information. You can get a copy of any police report from the police department for a modest fee. If there was no police report, contact the Department of Motor Vehicles. For a small fee, they will tell you who owns any vehicle for which you have a license number.*

Remember, when you sue more than one person (in this case the driver and the owner if they are different), you serve papers on both. When a business owns a vehicle, sue both the driver and the owners of the business.

G. SPECIAL PROCEDURES FOR SUITS AGAINST MINORS

It is very difficult to sue a minor for a breach of contract because minors can disavow (back out of) any contract they sign as long as they do it before they turn eighteen, unless the contract was for a necessity of life, i.e., food, in which case the parents are responsible.** You can sue minors for damage to your person or property. If you wish to do so, you must also list a parent or legal guardian on the court papers. You could do it like this:

"John Jefferey, a minor, and William Jefferey, his father."

It is very difficult to collect from minors themselves as most don't have money or income. Of course, there are exceptions to

---

* The D.M.V. will ask you why you want this information. Simply tell them "to file a lawsuit based on a motor vehicle accident". This is a legitimate reason and you will get the information you need. The owner of the car will, however, be notified of your request.

** An exception to this general rule that minors can disavow their contracts has to do with minors emancipated under Civil Code Sections 60–70. Minors who are on active duty in the armed services, are legally married or who have been emancipated by court order must stand behind their contracts as if they were adults.

this rule, but most minors are, almost by definition, broke. Thus, it doesn't usually pay to bother with suits against minors unless you can collect from the minor's parents. Normally a parent is not legally responsible to pay for damages done by his or her children. However, when a child is guilty of "willful misconduct", a parent can be liable up to $5,000 per act ($30,000 if a gun is involved). Parents are also liable for damage done by their minor children in auto accidents when they authorized the child to drive.

EXAMPLE 1: John Johnson, age 17, trips over his shoelace while delivering your newspaper and crashes through your glass door. Can you recover from John's parents? Probably not, as John is not guilty of "willful misconduct".

EXAMPLE 2: John shoots out the same glass door with a slingshot after you have repeatedly asked his parents to disarm him. Can you recover from the parents? Probably.

H. SPECIAL RULES FOR SUITS AGAINST CITY, COUNTY AND STATE

In California before you can sue a city because your car was illegally towed away or a city employee caused you damage, or for any other reason involving personal injury or property damage, you must first file a claim with the city and have it denied. Get a claim form from the city clerk. Your claim must be filed within 100 days of the date of the incident. The city attorney will review your claim and make a recommendation to the City Council. Sometimes the recommendation will be to pay you — most often it will be to deny your claim. Once the City Council acts, you will receive a letter. If it's a denial, take it with you when you file your Small Claims action. The clerk will want to see it.

The rules for suits against counties are basically the same. Get your complaint form from the clerk of the Board of Supervisors. Complete and file it within 100 days of the incident. Within a month or so after filing, you will be told whether your claim is approved or denied. If your claim is denied, you can then proceed to file in Small Claims Court.

Claims against the State of California must also be filed within 100 days for personal injury and property damage. Claims should be filed with the State Board of Control, Suite 300, 926 J Street, Sacramento, California 95814.

9

WHERE CAN I SUE?

Small Claims Court are local. This makes sense because the amounts involved aren't large enough to make it worthwhile to require people to travel great distances. A Small Claims Court judicial district covers an individual city, several cities, or a county. The next city or county will have its own similar, but separate, Small Claims Court. Normally, your dispute will be with a person or business located nearby. You can sue in the judicial district where the defendant resides or, if a corporation is involved, where its main place of business is located. Sometimes though, it is not so easy to understand where to file your suit. This might be the case if the person you wish to sue lives 100 (or 500) miles away, or has moved since the dispute arose.

On the first page of the first chapter we asked you to get a copy of the rules for your local Small Claims Court.* Refer to them now. The first thing you will wish to understand are the geographical boundaries of the Small Claims Court judicial district. If this information is not set out in the information sheet, call the clerk of the court and ask. You may be able to sue in more than one judicial district. If this is the case, choose the one that is most convenient to you.

---

* If your dispute arose at an area some distance from your home and the person you wish to sue also lives there, you will want the rules for this district.

Now let's look at the rules as to where you can sue in more detail:

A. YOU CAN SUE A PERSON OR BUSINESS WHERE HE, SHE OR IT RESIDES/DOES BUSINESS

This rule makes good sense, doesn't it? If a suit is brought where the defendant is located, he or she can't complain that it is unduly burdensome to appear. Books have been written about the technical definition of residence. Indeed, I remember with horror trying to sort out a law school exam in which the professor had given a person with numerous homes and businesses "contact" with six different judicial districts. The point of the examination was for us students to figure out where he could be sued. Thankfully, you don't have to worry about this sort of nonsense.*
If you believe a business or individual to be sufficiently present within a particular judicial district so that it would not be a hardship for them to appear in court there, go ahead and file your suit.

---

* The legal system as a whole and lawyers in particular would be better off if they moved to simplify procedures. Much of the present confusion seems to stem, not from common sense, but from a love of making what could be simple, more and more curious. Could it be that lawyers make more money when our judicial system resembles Alice's Wonderland?

The worst that can happen — and this is highly unlikely — is that the judge will tell you to start over someplace else.

EXAMPLE: Downhill Skier lives in the city, but also owns a mountain cabin where he spends several months a year. Late one snowy afternoon, Downhill drives his new Porsche from the ski slopes to his ultra-modern, rustic cabin. Turning into his driveway, he skids and does a bad slalom turn right into Woodsey Carpenter's 1957 International Harvester Pickup. Where can Woodsey sue? He can sue in the city where Downhill has his permanent address. He can probably also sue in the county where the cabin is located, on the theory that Downhill also lives there. But read on — as you will see under Section D below, it isn't necessary for Woodsey to even get into the residence question, as he can also sue in the mountain county on the theory that the injury occurred there.

NOTE: You can sue multiple defendants in any judicial district in which one resides even though the other(s) live in another part of the state.

B. THE CONTRACT WHICH IS THE BASIS OF YOUR SUIT WAS TO BE PERFORMED IN A PARTICULAR JUDICIAL DISTRICT

In addition to suing where the defendant resides, you can also sue at the place where an obligation (contract) was to be carried out. This, too, is good common sense as the law assumes that, if people agree to carry out a contract at a certain location, it is probably reasonably convenient to both. If, for example, Downhill gets a telephone installed in his cabin, or has the fender on his Porsche fixed, or has a cesspool put in, or agrees to sit for a portrait in the mountain county, he can be sued there if he fails to keep his part of the bargain. Of course, as we learned above, Downhill might also be sued in the city where he resides permanently.

EXAMPLE: John Gravenstein lives in Sonoma County, California, where he owns an apple orchard. He calls the Acme Mechanical Apple Picker Co., an international corporation with offices in San Francisco, New York, Paris and Guatemala City, and orders spare parts for his Acme apple picker. John deals with the San Francisco office. The parts are sent to John from San Francisco via

U.P.S. They turn out to be defective. After trying and failing to reach a settlement with Acme, John wants to know if he can sue them in Sonoma County. No. Acme doesn't reside in Sonoma County, and they performed no action there in connection with their agreement to sell John the spare parts. John would have to bring his claim in Small Claims Court in San Francisco. But now let's assume that John dealt with Acme's Sonoma County representative who came to his orchard to take the order and who later installed the defective machinery. Now John can sue locally since the contract was to be performed in Sonoma County.

REMINDER: You should now realize, that there are often several reasons why it can be OK to bring a suit in a particular place. You only need one, but it never hurts to have several. Also, as you should now understand, there may be two, three or more judicial districts in which you can file your case. In this situation, simply choose the one most convenient to you.

C. THE PERSON THAT YOU WISH TO SUE SIGNED A CONTRACT WITHIN A PARTICULAR JUDICIAL DISTRICT

This rule is similar to B just above, but it can be different. Suppose now a situation where John comes to Acme's office in San Francisco and signs the apple picker contract, with the equipment to be installed by Acme's local employee in Sonoma County. Assume that this time Acme keeps its part of the bargain, but John fails to pay. Where can Acme sue? Either in San Francisco where the contract was signed, or in Sonoma County where the contract was to be carried out. Also, as we learned in A above, Acme has another reason for being able to sue in Sonoma County — it's the place of John's residence.

Some large retailers used to put a clause in all of their contracts saying that, no matter where the contract was actually signed, the signature of the company didn't take effect until it was approved at the home office (often on the other side of the state). This was a gimmick, so that the company could sue everyone at the location of the company home office. People often couldn't defend themselves because it was impractical to show up in a court at the other end of the state. This practice is no longer legal. Now, the suit must be brought where the contract was actually signed by the defendant. If you feel that you are being cheated by this old hustle, call the State of California Attorney General's office and report the violators.

NOTE: If the person or corporation you wish to sue resided/did business in the judicial district at the time a contract was signed, you can sue them there even though they moved later and no longer reside in the judicial district at the time of the suit.

D. AN INJURY TO A PERSON OR TO HIS/HER PROPERTY OCCURRED WITHIN A PARTICULAR JUDICIAL DISTRICT

This means, quite simply, that, if you are in a car accident, a dog bites you, a tree falls on your noggin, or a neighbor floods your cactus garden, etc., you can sue in the judicial district where the injury occurred.

EXAMPLE: Downhill is returning to his home in San Francisco. He is driving his Porsche carefully, still thankful that no one was injured when he hit Woodsey. At the same time, John Gravenstein is rushing to the city to try and get spare parts for his still broken apple picker. John jumps a red light and crumples Downhill's other fender. The accident occurs in Marin county, a county in which neither John nor Downhill live. After parking his car and taking a taxi home, Downhill tries to figure out where he can sue if he can't work out a fair settlement with John. Unfortunately for him, he can't sue in San Francisco as John doesn't reside there and the accident occurred in Marin. Downhill would have to sue either in Marin County, where his property was damaged, or in Sonoma County, where John lives. Luckily for Downhill, Marin County adjoins San Francisco. Had the accident occurred in Los Angeles County, however, Downhill would have been put to a lot more trouble if he wished to sue.

E. SPECIAL RULES FOR RETAIL INSTALLMENT SALES CONTRACTS AND MOTOR VEHICLE FINANCE SALES

If your case involves a motor vehicle or a major piece of property such as a television or appliance that you bought on time, you may file suit where you presently live, where the vehicle or goods are permanently kept, where you lived when you entered into the contract or where you signed the contract.

10

PLAINTIFF'S AND DEFENDANT'S FILING FEES, COURT PAPERS AND COURT DATES

A. HOW MUCH DOES IT COST?

No state charges much for filing a case in Small Claims Court. The fee in California is $2.00 both for filing a "Claim of Plaintiff" and a "Claim of Defendant." There is an additional $3.00 fee for serving papers by certified mail on each defendant. You can recover your filing and service costs if you win (see Chapter 15).

B. FILLING OUT YOUR COURT PAPERS AND GETTING YOUR COURT DATE

Now let's look at the initial court papers themselves to be sure that you don't trip over a detail. Forms in use in California are all substantially the same although there are differences in detail in the different judicial districts. You should have little trouble filling out your papers by following the examples printed here but, if you do, simply ask the clerk for help. Small Claims clerks are required by law to give you as much help as possible short of practicing law (whatever that is). A friendly, courteous approach to the clerk can often result in much helpful information and advice.

Step 1 "The Plaintiff's Statement"

To start your case in Small Claims Court, go to the Small Claims clerk's office and fill out the form entitled "Plaintiff's Statement". If you have carefully read the first nine chapters of this book, this should be easy. Be particularly careful that you are suing in the right judicial district (Chapter 9) and that you are properly naming the defendant (Chapter 8).

SMALL CLAIMS COURT OF CALIFORNIA, COUNTY OF ALAMEDA

Andrew Printer,
Plaintiff(s) vs.

Acme Illusions, Inc.,
Defendant(s)

SMALL CLAIMS CASE NUMBER

PLAINTIFF'S STATEMENT

1. Please read carefully the instructions appearing below before filling out this form:
   a. If you are suing one or more individuals, give full name of each.
   b. If you are suing a business owned by an individual, give the name of the owner and the name of the business he owns.
   c. If you are suing a partnership, give the names of the partners and the name of the partnership.
   d. If you are suing a corporation, give its full name.
   e. If your claim arises out of a vehicle accident, the driver of the other vehicle must be named, and the registered owner of the other vehicle should also be named.

2. State your name and residence address, and the name and address of any other person joining with you in this action. If this claim arises from a business transaction, give the name and address of your business.

see ch. 7
   a. Name *Andrew Printer*
      Address *1800 Marilee St., Fremont, CA.* Phone No. *827-7000*
   b. Name _____
      Address _____ Phone No. _____

3. State the name and address of each person or business firm you are suing:

see ch. 8
   a. Name *Acme Illusions, Inc.*
      Address *100 Primrose Path, Oakland, CA.*
   b. Name _____
      Address _____
   c. Name _____
      Address _____

see ch. 4
4. State the amount you are claiming. $ *600.00*

5. Describe briefly the nature of your claim:

see ch. 2
   Failure to pay for printing and typesetting.

6. If your claim does not arise out of a vehicle accident, give address below where obligation was entered into or was to be performed or where injury was incurred.
   1800 Marilee St., *Fremont, CA.*
   (street address) (city or locality)

7. Fill out this section if your claim arises out of a vehicle accident:

see ch. 9
   a. Date on which accident occurred: _____ , 19_____ .
   b. Street or intersection and city or locality where accident occurred:
      _____

   c. If you are claiming damages to a vehicle, were you on the date of the accident the registered owner of that vehicle? _____
      (yes or no)

8. I have received and read the form entitled "Information to Plaintiff"
      Andrew Printer
      Signature

Step 2 "The Claim of Plaintiff"

When you have completed your "Plaintiff's Statement", give it to the court clerk who will then use it to type out your "Claim of Plaintiff" form and assign your case a number. You will be asked to sign this form under penalty of perjury. A copy of the "Claim of Plaintiff" will go to the judge and another must be served on the defendant (see Chapter 11). Here is a sample of the "Claim of Plaintiff" in use in Fremont, California.

MUNICIPAL COURT OF CALIFORNIA, SMALL CLAIMS DIVISION, COUNTY OF ALAMEDA

FREMONT-NEWARK-UNION CITY JUDICIAL DISTRICT
(415) 791-4680 39439 PASEO PADRE PARKWAY
DRAWER J. FREMONT 94537

NO SC _____

PLAINTIFF (Name and address)

Andrew Printer
1800 Marilee Street
Fremont, California 94536

DEFENDANT (Name and address of each)

Acme Illusions, Inc.
100 Primrose Path
Oakland, California 94602

CLAIM OF PLAINTIFF
AND ORDER

CLAIM OF PLAINTIFF

1 Defendant is indebted to plaintiff in the sum of $ 600.00 _____ not including court costs, for __failure to pay for printing and typesetting.__

2 Plaintiff has demanded that defendant pay this sum and it has not been paid

3 This court is the proper court for the hearing because

a ___ At least one defendant now resides or a corporate defendant does business in this judicial district.

b ___ Injury to person or damage to personal property occurred in this judicial district.

c _X_ Defendant entered into or signed in this judicial district a contract not involving a retail installment account or an auto finance sale.

d _X_ The obligation was to be performed in this judicial district on a contract not involving a retail installment account, an auto finance sale, or the furnishing of goods, services, or loans intended primarily for personal, family, or household use.

e ___ Defendant resided or a corporate defendant did business in this judicial district at the time the contract was entered into for the furnishing of goods, services or loans intended primarily for personal, family, or household use, and not involving a retail installment account or an auto finance sale

f ___ This action is on a retail installment account or contract (CC 1812 10), specify

g ___ This action is on a motor vehicle finance sale (CC 2984 4) specify

4 I have not previously filed this claim against the above named defendant(s)

5 I understand that

a Although I may consult an attorney I cannot be represented by an attorney at the trial in the small claims division,
b I must appear at the time and place for trial and have with me witnesses and evidence (Such as books, papers, receipts, and exhibits) to prove my claim,
c I have no right of appeal from a judgment on my claim

I declare (Certify) under penalty of perjury that the foregoing is true and correct and that this declaration is executed on

(Date) ___(fill in date)___ at (Place) __Fremont__ , California

ORDER

Andrew Printer
Signature of declarant

(for the clerk to fill in)

TO DEFENDANT If you wish to oppose plaintiff's claim you are directed to appear in the above entitled court in

Department _____ at _____ on _____

You should have with you any witnesses and evidence (Such as books, papers, receipts and exhibits) to establish your defense

IF YOU DO NOT APPEAR, THE COURT MAY AWARD PLAINTIFF THE AMOUNT FOUND TO BE DUE UPON PLAINTIFF'S CLAIM AND ALSO COSTS OF THE ACTION INCLUDING COST OF SERVICE OF THIS ORDER, WHICH COULD RESULT IN GARNISHMENT OF YOUR WAGES AND TAKING OF YOUR MONEY OR PROPERTY.

Dated _____ Clerk of the Municipal Court, by Deputy _____

Date				
Date _____	Hearing reset for _____	at ____	M., Dept. _____	
Date _____	Hearing reset for _____	at ____	M., Dept. _____	
Date _____	Hearing reset for _____	at ____	M., Dept. _____	
Date _____	Hearing reset for _____	at ____	M., Dept. _____	

FORM NO
170-128
REV 2/80

Date of Proceeding	Proceedings (applicable only when dated and/or checked in box)	FEES, COSTS, ETC	
		AMOUNT	RECEIPT NO
	Claim of Plaintiff Fees paid, order issued		
	Delivered to Plaintiff for personal service		
	Order and copy of declaration Mailed to defendant(s) by certified mail		

DOCKET COPY

The declaration under penalty of perjury must be signed in California, or in a state that authorizes use of a declaration in place of an affidavit, otherwise an affidavit is required

Step 3 Getting A Hearing Date

One of the great advantages of Small Claims Court is that disputes are settled quickly. This is important. Many people avoid lawyers and the regular courts primarily because they take forever to get a dispute settled. Business people, for example, increasingly rely on private arbitration, caring more that a dispute be resolved promptly than that they win a complete victory. Anyone who has had to wait two years for a case to be heard in some constipated state trial court knows through bitter experience that the old cliche, "justice delayed is justice denied", is all too true.

In California, Section 117d of the Code of Civil Procedure requires that, if the defendant resides in the same county in which the action is brought, the hearing should be no sooner than 10 days, or longer than 40 days from the time the papers are filed. If the defendant lives outside of the county where you bring suit, the case will be heard not less than 30, nor more than 70 days from the date you file your complaint. If there is more than one defendant, and one or more lives in the county where you file and one or more in another county, the case will be treated as if all defendants live within your county: that is, the case will be heard within 30 days of the time the papers are filed.

When you file your papers, you should also arrange with the clerk for a court date. Get a date that is convenient for you. You need not take the first date the clerk suggests. Be sure to leave yourself enough time to get a copy of the "Claim of Plaintiff" form served on the defendant(s). (See Chapter 11 for service information.) If you fail to properly serve your papers on the defendant in time, there is no big hassle — just notify the clerk, get a new court date, and try again.

Small Claims Courts are most often held at 9:00 A.M. on working days. Some judicial districts are beginning to hold evening and Saturday sessions. Ask the clerk for a schedule. If evening and Saturday sessions aren't available, why not?

C. THE DEFENDANT'S FORMS

No papers need be filed to defend a case in Small Claims Court. You just show up on the date and at the time indicated, ready to tell your side of the story. If you need to get the hearing delayed, see Section E below. It is proper, and advisable, for a defendant to call or write the plaintiff and see if a fair settlement can be reached without going to court (see Chapter 6).

Sometimes someone sues you in a situation where you were planning to sue them (i.e., a traffic accident where you each believe the other is at fault). As long as your grievance stems from the same incident, you can file a "Claim of Defendant" for up to $750 in Small Claims Court and have it heard by a judge at the same time that the plaintiff's claim against you is considered.* However, if you believe that the plaintiff owes you money as the result of a different injury or breach of contract, you must file your own separate case.

But what happens if you wish to make a claim against the plaintiff for more than $750? First re-read Chapter 4 and decide whether you want to scale down your claim to fit into Small Claims. If you don't, you must file your claim in either justice or Municipal Court (up to $15,000) or Superior Court (over $15,000) and pay all necessary filing fees. Your next step is to file an affidavit setting forth the facts of the higher court action with the Small Claims Court clerk. This must be done prior to the hearing date for the Small Claims Court case and costs $1.00. In addition, a copy of this affidavit must be delivered to the plaintiff in person. Now it's up to the judge. Section 116.8 of the Code of Civil Procedure states:

> "The Small Claims Court shall not transfer the Small Claims Court action to the court set forth in the affidavit until a judgment is rendered in the Small Claims Court action, unless the ends of justice would be served by such a prejudgment transfer of the proceedings ... If the Small Claims matter is transferred prior to judgment, both actions shall be tried together in the transferred court."

NOTE: If you have a claim against a plaintiff for an amount less than the Small Claims Court maximum which arises out of the same transaction or situation that forms the basis of his or her suit against you, you are required to file it prior to the time that the plaintiff's case is heard. If you fail to file and let the case be decided, you will not be permitted to file at a later time.

---

* When you file a "Claim of Defendant", you become a plaintiff as far as this claim is concerned. This means that, if you lose, you can't appeal because plaintiffs can't appeal. Of course, if you lose on the original plaintiff's claim, you can appeal that portion of the judgment (see Chapter 22).

Name, Address and Telephone No. of Defendant(s) | Space Below for use of Court Clerk Only

Acme Illusions, Inc.
100 Primrose Path
Oakland, California 94602

SMALL CLAIMS COURT OF CALIFORNIA, COUNTY OF ALAMEDA

Andrew Printer
_____
Plaintiff(s)

No.   SC

VS.

CLAIM OF DEFENDANT

Acme Illusions, Inc.
_____
Defendant(s)
(abbreviated title)

I, the undersigned, defendant and claimant in the above-entitled action say that the plaintiff is indebted to me in the sum of $ 300.00 _____ for delays and poor workmanship in printing job _____

which amount I pray be allowed against the plaintiff herein.

Executed on _____ (Date) _____ at _____ Oakland _____, California.
                (date)

I declare under penalty of perjury that the foregoing is true and correct.

Walto Fergus, President
Signature of defendant

DECLARATION OF SERVICE

I served the within Claim by delivering to and leaving with the person or persons personally, hereinafter named, a copy thereof, at the address and on the date set forth opposite each name of said person or persons, in the County of Alameda _____, State of California, to wit:

Name of Person Served*	Street Address and City where Served	Date of Service
Andrew Printer	1800 Marilee St., Fremont, CA.	(Date)

Fee for Service $ 8.00 _____, Mileage $_____. Total $ 8.00 _____

Executed on _____ (Date) _____, at _____ Oakland _____, California.
                (date)   (place)

I declare under penalty of perjury that the foregoing is true and correct.

Robert Rooster
Signature of Declarant

*If service is upon a corporation, partnership, or association, state its name and the name and official title of person to whom copy is delivered.

JUDGEMENT ON CLAIM OF DEFENDANT	
Judgment for Claimant $	
Stay _____ days	Costs $ _____
Dated: _____	

D. CHANGING A COURT DATE

It is sometimes impossible for a defendant to be present on the day ordered by the court for the hearing. It can also happen that the plaintiff will pick out a court date and get the defendant served only to find that an unexpected emergency makes it impossible for him or her to be present.

It is normally not difficult to get a case delayed. To arrange this, call the other party and see if you can agree on a mutually convenient date. Don't call the clerk first — they don't know what days the other party has free. Sometimes it is difficult to face talking to someone who you are involved in a lawsuit with, but you will just have to swallow your pride and start dialing. Once all parties have agreed to a new date, notify the court clerk in writing with the signatures of both parties. Here is a sample:

```
                                    11 South Street
                                    San Diego, CA
                                    January 10, 19___

Clerk of the Small Claims Court
San Diego, California
                                    Re: SC 4117 Rodriguez v. McNally
Dear Clerk:

Mr. Rodriguez and I agree to request that you postpone this case to a
date after March 1, 19___.


                                    _____
                                    JOHN McNALLY


                                    _____
                                    JOHN RODRIGUEZ
```

If you speak to the other party(ies) and find that he or she is completely uncoopertive, put your request for a delay (continuance) in writing, along with the circumstances that make it impossible for you keep the first date. Send your letter to the judge of the Small Claims Court. Here is a sample:

```
                                    37 Birdwalk Blvd.
                                    Occidental, Calif.

                                    January 10, 19___

Judge John Justice
Small Claims Court
City Hall
San Francisco, Calif.           Re: Small Claims No. 374-628

Dear Judge Justice:

    I have been served with a complaint (No. 374-628) by John's Laundry,
Inc.  The date set for a hearing, February 15, falls on the day of my
son's graduation from Nursing School in Oscaloosa, Oklahoma, which my
husband and I plan to attend.

    I called John's Laundry and asked to have the case delayed one week.
They just laughed and said that they would not give me any cooperation.
```

F. IF ONE PARTY DOESN'T SHOW UP

If one party to a case doesn't appear in court on the proper day
at the proper time, the case is normally decided in favor of the
other. Depending on whether it is the plaintiff or defendant who
fails to show up, the terms used by the judge to make his decision
are different. If the plaintiff appears, but the defendant doesn't, a
"default judgment" is normally entered in favor of the plaintiff
(see Chapters 12 and 15 for more information on defaults). Occasionally, although it happens far less frequently, it is the plaintiff
who fails to show up. In this situation, the judge will dismiss the
case.

If you are the person who failed to show up (whether defendant or plaintiff) and you still want a chance to argue the case on
its merits, you must act immediately, or forever hold your peace.

1. Setting Aside A Default (Defendant's Remedy)

Courts are not very sympathetic to setting aside or vacating a
default judgment to allow a defense to be made unless you can
show that the original papers weren't properly served on you and
that you didn't know about the hearing. This can happen if someone signs your name for the certified letter and then doesn't give it
to you, or because a dishonest process server doesn't serve you,
but tells the court he did, or for some other reason. As soon as you
find out that a default judgment has been entered against you, call
the court clerk. It doesn't make any difference if the hearing you
missed was months before as long as you move to set it aside
immediately upon learning about it.

If you have had a default judgment entered against you after
you were properly served, you will face an uphill struggle to get it
set aside. Some judges will accept excuses such as "I forgot", "I

was sick", "I got called out of town", etc., and some will not. Generally, judges assume that you could have at least called, or had a friend call, no matter what the emergency. However, if you act promptly (this means within 30 days after the default), and if you have a good excuse, you stand a reasonable chance of getting the judge to set the default aside* (C.C.P. 117.8(b)).

NOTE: You can't appeal from a default judgment even if you have a great case. You must try to get the default set aside or the judgment will be final. To try to set aside a default, go to the Small Claims clerk's office and ask for the proper form. If the Small

---

* If the defendant was not properly served and did not appear at the hearing in the Small Claims Court, the defendant has 180 days to move to vacate after he or she discovers or should have discovered that judgment was entered against him or her (C.C.P. Section 117.8(d)).

Claims Court denies your motion to vacate the judgment after you have appeared in court or submitted a written justification, you may appeal as to this denial.

211-147

COUNTY OF ALAMEDA, STATE OF CALIFORNIA

Andrew Printer .... vs Acme Illusions, Inc. ....
Plaintiff(s)   Defendant(s)

ACTION NO. (Fill in)

DECLARATION AND NOTICE OF MOTION TO VACATE JUDGMENT

I, the undersigned, say: I am the President of Defendant Corp the above entitled action; that judgment was entered on (Fill in date) ...., 19........ against Acme Illusions, Inc.

I was not present at the trial and did not notify the court before trial that I could not be present because.............. A death in the family made it impossible to do so

I believe I can prove the following facts to support my case, to wit: that Acme Illusions is not .... indebted to Andrew Printer because the printing work was improperly done

WHEREFORE, I request that said judgment be vacated and the case be tried on its merits.

I declare under penalty of perjury that the foregoing is true and correct.

Executed on (Date) ...., at Oakland, California.

Waldo Fergus
Signature of Declarant

NOTICE OF MOTION

(To be filled in by the clerk)

To ...., ... (address)

Please take notice that on ...., 19........, at .... M., in Dept. Two

of the above entitled court, 2120 Grove Street, Berkeley, California, ...

will move the court for an order vacating the judgment heretofore entered in this case and for trial forthwith.

Dated ...., 19.........

....
Deputy Clerk

---

2. Vacating A Judgment Of Dismissal (Plaintiff's Remedy)

Vacating a judgment of dismissal is even more difficult than setting aside a default. Why? Because the plaintiff is the one who started the case and arranged for the court date. The judge assumes that the plaintiff should be able to show up for his or her own case, or at least, call the court clerk prior to the court date and explain why he or she can't appear.

However, now and then emergencies happen, or someone simply makes a mistake about the day. Judges can, and do, vacate dismissals if both the following circumstances exist. One, the plaintiff moves to have the judgment vacated "immediately" upon learning of his mistake. "Immediately" never is interpreted to be more than 20 days from the day the dismissal is entered and is thought by most judges to be a much shorter time. Two, the plaintiff has a good explanation as to why he was unable to be present or call on the day the case was regularly scheduled. A judge might accept something like this: "I had a flu with a high fever and simply lost track of a couple of days. As soon as I felt better, which was two days after my case was dismissed, I came to the clerk's office to try to get this case re-scheduled."

To get a judgment vacated, you must fill out the same form as the one set out in Section 1, just above.

11

SERVING YOUR PAPERS

After you have filed your "Claim of Plaintiff" form with the clerk following the instructions in Chapter 10 B, a copy must be served on the person, persons, or corporation you are suing. This is called "service of process". Your lawsuit is not complete without it. The reason that you must serve the other side is simple — the person(s) you are suing are entitled to be notified of the general nature of your claim and the day, time and place when they can show up to defend themselves.

A. WHO MUST BE SERVED

All defendants that you list on your "Claim of Plaintiff" should be served. It is not enough to serve one defendant and assume that he or she will tell the other(s). This is true even if the defendants are married, or living together. If you don't serve a particular defendant, the court can't enter a judgment against that person. If you sue more than one person and can serve only one, a judge can enter a judgment against the person served, in effect dropping your action against the other defendant(s).

B. HOW TO SERVE YOUR PAPERS

There are several approved ways to serve papers. All depend on your knowing where the defendant is. If you can't find the defendant, you can't serve him and it makes little sense to file a lawsuit.

Method 1 Personal Service:

Any person who is eighteen years of age, or older, except the person bringing a suit or a witness may serve the defendant by handing him the "Claim of Plaintiff" any place in California.* Any person means just that — you can hire the county sheriff or marshal (often good for its sobering effect), or a private process server (listed in the Yellow Pages), or you can have a friend or relative do the service. Only you or someone whom you plan to call as a witness can't serve the papers in your lawsuit.

The "Claim of Plaintiff" must be handed to the defendant personally. You can't simply leave the paper at his or her job, or home, or in the mailbox. A person making a service who doesn't know the person involved should make sure that he or she is serving the right person. If a defendant refuses to take the paper, acts hostile or attempts to run away, the process server should simply put the paper down and leave. Valid service has been accomplished. The process server should never try to use force to get a defendant to take any papers.

Method 2 By Certified Mail:

You can also serve your "Claim of Plaintiff" by certified mail. The clerk of the court does the mailing for you. The fee in California is $3.00 for each defendant. This is recoverable if you win (see Chapter 15 C). The mail method is both cheap and easy, but it depends for its success on the defendant signing for the letter. Most businesses and many individuals routinely sign to accept mail. However, some people never do, knowing instinctively, or perhaps from past experience, that nothing good ever comes by certified mail. I have asked several court clerks for an estimate as to the percentage of certified mail services that are

---

* Papers cannot validly be served out-of-state, unless they are for a case involving a motor vehicle accident. There is an interstate procedure for service on vehicle accidents through the Department of Motor Vehicles. The Small Claims Court clerk will show you how to accomplish this.

accepted. The consensus is 50%. If you try using the mail to serve your papers and fail, simply get a process server. Chances are the defendant will end up paying for it.

NOTE: Never assume that your certified mail service has been accomplished and show up in court on the day of the court hearing. If the defendant didn't sign for the paper, you will be wasting your time. Call the clerk a couple of days in advance and find out if the service of process has been completed.

Method 3 Substituted Service (or "Nail and Mail"):

Often it is hard to serve particular individuals. Some people have developed avoiding the process server into a high (but silly) art. In California and some other states, this no longer works as there is now a procedure which allows "substituted service."* It works like this in California:

If a person can't be served with "reasonable diligence," which is normally interpreted to be three unsuccessful tries at personal service, the papers may be served by leaving a copy of the summons and complaint at the person's dwelling place in the presence of a competent member of the household who is at least 18 years of age and who must be told what the papers are about *and* thereafter mailing a copy of the summons and complaint by first class mail to the person served. Service is complete ten days after mailing. Be sure that all steps are carried out by a disinterested adult. Because some Small Claims Court clerks interpret the requirement for "due diligence" differently, you will wish to run through the procedure with your local clerk before trying it. If your suit is against a corporation, the substituted service procedure is easier. There is no requirement that you try personal service three times before using substituted service. Papers may be served by leaving a copy of the summons and complaint at the defendant's office with a person apparently in charge of the office during normal business hours and then mailing another copy of the summons and complaint to the person to be served at the same address by first class mail. Service is accomplished ten days after mailing.

After service is accomplished, you must return an affidavit to the court clerk that all proper steps have been accomplished. See Section F, below.

---

* See California Code of Civil Procedure Section 415.20.

Method 4 For Serving Subpoenas Only:

In Chapter 14 we discuss subpoenaing witnesses and documents. Subpoenas can't be served by mail. They must be served by personal service. The rules as to who can do the serving, etc., are the same as those set forth above in Method 1. There is an important added requirement, however. The person making the service must be ready to pay the person subpoenaed a $12.00 witness fee on the spot if it is requested. If you hire a sheriff or marshal to do the service, he will ask you to pay this $12.00 fee, plus his service fee in advance. If the witness doesn't ask for the $12.00, it will be returned to you.

C. COSTS OF PERSONAL SERVICE

Professional process servers commonly charge from $8-$20 per service depending on the time and mileage involved.* You can usually get your costs of service added to your judgment if you win, but be sure to remind the judge to do this when you conclude your court presentation. However, a few courts such as the Berkeley Small Claims Court will not give the successful party an award of costs for a process server, unless they have first tried to have the papers served by the cheaper certified mail approach (Method 2 above). Other judicial districts such as Los Angeles prefer that you don't use the mail approach at all because they feel that too often the mail isn't accepted. Ask the Small Claims clerk in your district how they prefer that you accomplish service and how much the judge will allow as a service of process fee.

D. TIME LIMITS IN WHICH PAPERS MUST BE SERVED

The defendant is entitled to receive service of the "Claim of Plaintiff" form at least five days before the date of the court hearing, if he or she is served within the county in which the courthouse is located. If the defendant is served in a county other than the one where the trial is to take place, he must be served at least 15 days before the trial date.

If the defendant is served less than the required number of days before the trial date, he can either go ahead with the trial anyway, or request that the case be delayed (continued) for 10 to 30 days. If it is impossible to show up in person to ask for a delay, call the court clerk (telegraph if you can't call) and point out that you weren't served in the proper time and that you want the case put over. The clerk will see that a default judgment is not entered against you. See Chapter 10 E.

To count the days to see if service has been accomplished in the correct time, do not count the day the service is accomplished or the day of the court appearance. Do count weekends and holidays. Thus, if Jack served Julie on July 11 in Los Angeles County, with a "Declaration and Order" listing a July 17 court

---

* County officials such as sheriffs and marshals will only serve papers in the county in which they are located. Call them to ask about fees.

date in the same county, service would be proper. This is true even if Saturday and Sunday fell on July 14 and 15. To count the days you would not count July 11, the day of service, or July 17, the court date, but would count July 12, 13, 14, 15 and 16 for a total of five days. If you are unable to serve the defendant(s) within the proper time, simply ask the court clerk for a new court date and try again.

DEFENDANT'S NOTE: If you are improperly served either because you are not given adequate time, or the papers weren't handed to you personally, or a certified letter wasn't signed for by you, it is still wise for you to call the court clerk or show up in court on the day in question. Why should you have to do this if service was improper? Because the plaintiff may succeed in getting the case heard as a default if you fail to show up. It's more trouble to get a default set aside than to protect yourself from the start. But isn't this a Catch-22? You are entitled to proper service, but if you don't get it, you have to show up in court anyway? Perhaps, but as Catch-22's go, this one is mild. You can call the clerk or show up in court and request that the judge grant you a continuance to prepare your case. If the original service was in fact improper, your request will be honored. Of course, if you were improperly served and simply want to get the hearing out of the way, you can show up and go ahead with your case.

E. SERVING A BUSINESS

If you are suing someone who owns his own business, or is a partner in the business, you must serve the person individually using the rules set out above. However, if you are suing a corporation, the rules are a little different.

Although a corporation is a legal person for purposes of lawsuits, you will still need to have your papers served on someone who lives and breathes. This is true whether you have the papers served personally, or use certified mail.* The flesh and blood person should be an officer of the corporation (president, vicepresident, secretary or treasurer). Simply call the corporation and ask who, and where, they are. If they won't tell you, the city or county business tax and license people should be able to, at least

---

* In Los Angeles and some other California judicial districts, the clerks insist that you use personal service to serve a corporation.

for local corporations (see Chapter 8). If you have trouble getting someone at a large national corporation to accept service, call or write the California Secretary of State, Corporate Status Unit, 111 Capitol Mall, Sacramento, California 95814. They will be able to tell you who is authorized to accept service for the company in California. If you are suing a corporation in a situation where you know that the officers (or general manager) of the corporation work out of a local office, it is easy to use substituted service as set out in Method 3 above.

F. NOTIFYING THE COURT THAT SERVICE HAS BEEN ACCOMPLISHED ("PROOF OF SERVICE")

Where certified mail is involved, you need do nothing. The court clerk sends out the certified mail for you and the signed post office receipt comes back directly to the clerk if service is accomplished. It's as simple as that.

However, a court has no way of knowing whether or not papers have been successfully served by personal service unless you tell them. This is done by filing a piece of paper known as a "Proof of Service" with the court clerk after the service has been made. The "Proof of Service" is a small, perforated, tear-off form that is part of the "Declaration and Order" package which must be signed by the person actually making the service. A "Proof of Service" is used both by the plaintiff and by the defendant if he files a "counterclaim". It must be returned to the clerk's office not less than 48 hours before the trial. A "Proof of Service" is used when any legal documents are served by personal service. We will refer back to this example several times in future chapters.

G. SERVING A "CLAIM OF DEFENDANT"

As you will remember from our discussion in Chapter 9, a "Claim of Defendant" is the form that the defendant files when he wishes to sue the plaintiff for money damages arising out of the same incident that forms the basis for the plaintiff's suit. A "Claim of Defendant" should be filed with the clerk and served on the plaintiff at least five days prior to the time that the court has set for the hearing on the plaintiff's claim.* There will not be time to serve the "Claim of Defendant" by mail, so you will have to use personal service, returning a "Proof of Service" form to the court clerk. If you are a defendant who has filed a claim and you are unable to serve the plaintiff, simply show up at the court hearing date with your papers and serve the plaintiff in the hallway (not the courtroom). Then explain to the judge why it was impossible to locate the plaintiff earlier. The judge will either put the whole case over a few days, or allow you to proceed with your claim that day. Either way, he/she will accept your "Claim of Defendant" as validly served.

H. SERVING SOMEONE IN THE MILITARY — DECLARATION OF NON-MILITARY SERVICE

It is proper to serve someone who is on active duty in the armed forces. If he/she shows up, fine. If he/she doesn't, you have a problem. We learned in Chapter 10 that as a general rule, if a properly served defendant doesn't show up, you can get a "default judgment" against him or her. This is not true if the person you are suing is in the military (the reserves don't count).

Default judgments cannot normally be taken against people in the armed forces because Congress has given our military personnel special protections. To get a default judgment against any defendant a statement must be filed under penalty of perjury that he or she is not in the military. The "Declaration of Non-Military Service" is part of your "Claim of Plaintiff" package and is routinely filled out and signed as part of every case, unless, of course, the defendant is in the military. Clerks accept "Declaration of Non-Military Service" signed by the plaintiff, as long as the plaintiff reasonably believes that the defendant is not on active

---

* If the plaintiff has served the defendant less than 10 days before the date of the court hearing, the claim of defendant need only be served on the plaintiff one day prior to the hearing. C.C.P. 116.8.

duty. This constitutes a lenient interpretation of the law by clerks, but no one seems to be complaining.

CLAIM OF PLAINTIFF
DECLARATION OF NON-MILITARY SERVICE

I, the undersigned, say: that defendant(s)

_____

_____

and each of them, if more than one is named herein, is not now a person in the military service of the UNITED STATES as defined in Section 101 and sub-divisions thereof, of the Soldiers' and Sailors' Civil Relief Act of 1940, as amended, and not entitled to the benefits of said act, as amended:

I declare under penalty of perjury that the foregoing is true and correct.

Executed on _____ at _____ , Calif.
          (DATE)   (PLACE)

_____
(SIGNATURE OF DECLARANT)

12

THE DEFENDANT'S OPTIONS

This chapter is devoted to a review of the concerns of the defendant. Most of this material has already been discussed in the first eleven chapters, but it will be helpful to pull it all together in one place. Let's start by assuming that you are the person being sued. How do you approach what's happening to you? First, when you receive the plaintiff's papers, you will have to make one of several decisions. There is no one correct course of action — it all depends on your circumstances.

A. IMPROPER SERVICE

You may conclude that the service was not proper (see Chapter 11). Perhaps the "Claim of Plaintiff" was left with your neighbors, or maybe you didn't have the correct number of days in which to respond. You may be tempted not to show up in court, figuring that since you weren't served properly, the case can't be heard. As noted, this is not a smart idea if you wish to defend the case. The judge can easily be unaware of, or overlook, the service problem and issue a default judgment against you. If this happens, you will have to go to the trouble of requesting that the default be set aside. You are better off to contact the clerk, explain the problem with the service and ask that the case be continued to a date that is convenient to you. If the clerk can't help, write the judge or show up on the day in question and request a continuance.

B. NO DEFENSE

Now let's assume that the service was OK, but you have no real defense, or don't have the time to defend yourself, or for some other reason don't feel like going to court.* A decision not to show up will very likely result in a default judgment being entered against you. It will most probably be for the dollar amount demanded by the plaintiff, plus his or her filing fee and costs to serve you. We discuss default judgments in more detail in Chapters 10 and 15. Basically, a default judgment has the same effect as if you showed up, argued your case and lost.

If you do not dispute the plaintiff's claim, but cannot afford to pay it all at once, see Item 3 on the reverse side of the Claim of Plaintiff form that was served on you. Check the box and fill in the information. When the judge enters a judgment against you, he or she has the power to order that you pay in monthly installments and probably will do so.

C. TRY TO COMPROMISE

If you feel that perhaps the plaintiff has some right on his or her side, but that you are being sued for too much, contact the plaintiff and try to work out a compromise settlement. Any settlement you make should be set down in writing along the lines outlined in Chapter 6. It should also include a specific statement that the plaintiff will forever drop his pending lawsuit. Simply add a clause like the following to the sample agreement outlined in Chapter 6.

"As part of this settlement, _____(name of plaintiff)_____

---

* Many people are tempted not to show up and defend a case in Small Claims Court because they have no money and figure that even if they lose, the plaintiff can't collect. This is "grasshopper thinking". The sun may be shining today and the judgment may cause you no immediate problem. But remember, judgments are good for 10 years and can be renewed for another 10. You may put a few nickels together sometime in the future and you probably won't want them taken away by an industrious little ant holding a Small Claims judgment in his mouth. So wake up and defend yourself while you can.

hereby agrees to drop the lawsuit, number ___(insert number)
filed in Small Claims Court in the _____
judicial district on _____(date)_____
against _____(name of defendant)_____
and that no further court actions(s) will be filed regarding
the subject matter of this agreement."

As a practical matter any lawsuit that is not actively prosecuted will be dropped by the clerk. The reason that you want to have a settlement agreement written out is to cover the unlikely possibility that the other party will accept money from you and then try to go ahead with his suit too. If this happens, you need only show your written settlement agreement to the judge.

D. FIGHT BACK

Now we get to those of you who feel that you don't owe the plaintiff a dime. You will want to actively fight. This means that you must show up in court on the date stated in the papers served on you unless you get the case continued (see Chapter 10). A defendant need not file any papers with the court clerk; showing up ready to defend yourself is enough. The strategies to properly argue a case, including the presentation of witnesses, estimates, diagrams, etc. are discussed in Chapters 13-22 and apply equally to defendants and plaintiffs. You will wish to study this information carefully and develop a strategy for your case. You will also want to see whether the plaintiff has brought the case within the time allowed by the Statute of Limitations (Chapter 5) and whether he has asked for a reasonable amount of money (Chapter 4). If you simply show up without thinking out a coherent presentation, you are likely to lose.

E. FILE A "CLAIM OF DEFENDANT"

Finally, there are those of you who not only want to dispute the plaintiff's claim, but also want to sue him. This involves promptly filing a "Claim of Defendant" for up to $750 in Small Claims Court, or for a larger amount in Municipal or Superior Court. See Chapter 10 C and 11 G for more details.

13

GETTING READY FOR COURT

Once you have your papers on file and the defendant(s) served, the preliminaries are over and you are ready for the main event — your day in court. Movies, and especially T.V., have done much to make court proceedings false. Ask yourself, what was a trial like before every lawyer fancied himself Raymond Burr or Charles Laughton and judges acted "fatherly", or "stern", or "indignantly outraged"?

There are people whose lives revolve around courthouses, and who have been playing movie parts for so long that they have become caricatures of one screen star or another. Lawyers are particularly susceptible to this virus. All too often they substitute posturing and theatrics for good hard preparation. Thankfully though, most people who work in our courts quickly recover from movieitis and realize that the majestic courtroom is in truth a large, drafty hall with a raised platform at one end: His honor is only a lawyer dressed in a black shroud who knew the right politician and that they themselves are not bit players in "Witness For The Prosecution", "Inherit The Wind" or "Twelve Angry Men".

I mention movieitis because it's a common ailment in Small Claims Court. Cases that should be easily won are often lost because somebody goes marching around the courtroom antagonizing everyone with comic opera imitations of E. G. Marshall. And don't just assume that you are immune. Movieitis is a subtle disease because people often don't realize they have it. Ask yourself a few self-diagnostic questions. Have you watched courtroom scenes on T.V. or in the movies? Have you ever imagined that you were one of the actor-lawyers? How many times have you been in a real courtroom in comparison to watching movie set courtrooms?

My purpose here is not to lecture you on how to present yourself in court. But perhaps I can get you to remember something that you already know — you don't need to be false to yourself to succeed in Small Claims Court. You don't need to put on fancy clothes or airs, or try to appear more polished, intelligent or sophisticated than you are. Be yourself and you will do just fine. If you have a chance, go to the court a few days before your case is heard and watch for an hour or two. You may not learn a great deal that will be helpful in your case, but you will be a lot more relaxed and comfortable when your turn comes. Watching a few cases is a particularly good thing to do if you feel anxious about your court appearance. For those of you who love to act, who simply can't pass up an opportunity to perform, at least act real. That's right, go ahead and act if you must, but make your performance that of a person — not a personality.

Movieitis aside, most people I have watched in Small Claims Court have done extremely well. Many mornings I have been inspired, feeling that for the first time in years I have seen honesty and truth put in an appearance before the Bar of Justice. This truly surprised me as I had hardly ever taken the time to watch a Small Claims case before doing research for this book. I stopped taking clients several years ago, in part, because I hated the dishonest sham that goes on in the courtroom — hated the endless natterings between lawyers about logic-chopping technicalities while clients paid and paid and paid. It was wonderful to see that once the lawyers were removed and people began communicating directly, there was much about our court system that made sense.

Commonly a judge must decide a case, at least in part, on the basis of who seems to be the most believable. This is because there isn't enough hard evidence to be conclusive either way.

Different judges have varying prejudices, hunches, feelings, etc., about who is, or isn't, telling the truth. Often they themselves can't explain the many intangibles that go into making this sort of decision, but most agree that the more honestly a person presents himself/herself, the more likely he or she is to be believed. For example, a house painter who shows up in his overalls and puts his lunchbox under the chair will probably be much more convincing (and comfortable) than he would be if he came painfully squeezed into his blue wedding and funeral suit. As one judge told me, "A pimp being a pimp has as good a chance as anyone else in my courtroom, but a pimp who tries to act like Saint Paul better watch out."

Before we get into a discussion of how to prepare and present different types of cases, here are a few general suggestions:

A. INTERPRETER SERVICES

The Small Claims Court clerk is required to maintain and make available a list of interpreters in as many languages as possible who are willing to aid parties for no fee or a reasonable fee. However, failure to have an interpreter for a particular language on the list shall not invalidate any proceedings. C.C.P. 117.16.

B. PRE-TRIAL SETTLEMENT CONFERENCES

In the last several years, experimental legislation has resulted in optional pretrial conference procedures in San Jose, Los Angeles, and San Diego. As of this writing, most of these programs have been discontinued for lack of funds. Ask your local clerk if there is such a program in your area. If there is, it will operate something like this. Plaintiffs and defendants are given a chance to get together with a local lawyer to see if they can arrive at a compromise settlement. If this is not possible, plaintiff and defendant may be given a chance to present their case to a lawyer acting as judge in a proceeding less formal than the normal courtroom proceeding. It is too early to say for sure how these programs are working. However, I am extremely worried and cynical about the introduction of lawyers into the Small Claims process.* One of the main advantages of Small Claims has been to get away from lawyers and every time I think of them starting to get involved in Small Claims, I think of what eventually happened when the Arab let the camel put his nose in the tent. If you are in Los Angeles, San Jose or San Diego and want more information about their conciliation programs, contact the Small Claims Court clerk.

C. GETTING TO THE COURTHOUSE

Before you get to the right courtroom, you have to get to the right building. Small Claims Courts are often not in the main courthouse, but like a half forgotten stepsister, are housed wherever there's an empty room. Don't assume that you know where to go if you haven't been there before. Plaintiffs have already had to find the clerk's office, so they probably know where the courtroom is, but defendants should check this out. Be sure too, that your witnesses know exactly where and when to show up. And do plan to be on time — people who rush in flustered and late start with a strike against them.**

NOTE: San Francisco and some other counties use an insulting hurry-up-and-wait technique that would make the Army blush. They have everyone show up at 8:15 A.M. in one large room. At this time the judges are still home having coffee. Court is supposed to start at 9:00, although 9:15 is normal, and 9:30 all too common. Can you imagine the court making lawyers show up an hour early for no reason? Courts never start before 9:00 in the morning — if they tell you an earlier time, call them up and ask what time the judge really gets there.

D. UNDERSTANDING THE COURTROOM

Most Small Claims proceedings are conducted in standard

---

* The California Bar Association has supported legislation adding lawyers to the Small Claims process and many lawyers in the legislature have been involved in its passage. I believe that it is a serious conflict of interest for lawyer-legislators to vote on Small Claims bills, especially when the effect is to make more jobs for lawyers. As I discuss in Chapter 25, I believe that arbitration and mediation approaches would be helpful in Small Claims Court, but why not have them provided by non-lawyers?

** Most Small Claims Courts are held at 9:00 A.M., but there is a slow movement toward night and Saturday sessions. Check locally to see if night and Saturday sessions exist in your area. If not, why not?

courthouses that are also used for other purposes. Indeed, sometimes you will have to sit through a few minutes of some other type of court proceeding before the Small Claims calendar is called.

Most judges still sit on high in their little, wooden throne boxes, and most still wear those depressing black judicial robes that trace their history back over a thousand years to an England in which courts were largely controlled by king, nobility and clergy. There are no laws requiring these out-of-date traditions, and a few judges prefer to conduct their court more informally. In addition to the judge, a clerk and a bailiff will normally be present. They sit at tables immediately in front of the judge. The clerk's job is to keep the judge supplied with necessary files and papers, and to make sure that proceedings flow smoothly. A clerk is not the same as a court reporter who keeps a word-by-word record of proceedings. No such record is kept in Small Claims Court, and no court reporter is present.

Courtrooms are divided about two-thirds of the way toward the front by a little fence. This fence is known to initiates as the "bar". The public must stay on the opposite side of the bar from the

THE JUDGE: IDENTIFIES THE PEOPLE INVOLVED. HEARS TESTIMONY. LOOKS AT DOCUMENTS AND DECIDES THE CASE.

THE ROBE: HIGH FASHION IN THE MIDDLE AGES. PERHAPS A BIT SILLY TODAY, BUT SEEMS TO MAKE THE JUDGE FEEL IMPORTANT.

THE CLERK: ANNOUNCES THE CASE. COLLECTS AND MARKS THE DOCUMENTARY EVIDENCE.

THE BALIFF GENERALLY DOES NOTHING, BUT IS PRESENT TO PRESERVE ORDER.

THE COURT ROOM.

JUDGE

BAILIFF: MAY BE SEATED OR STANDING

CLERK:

JUDGES BENCH

WITNESS STAND: RARELY USED IN SMALL CLAIMS COURT.

COUNSEL TABLE BOTH PARTIES AND THE WITNESSES SIT HERE FACING THE JUDGE.

THE BAR: SEPARATES THE PROFESSIONALS FROM THE GENERAL PUBLIC.

AUDIENCE SEATING: THE PUBLIC SECTION OF THE COURTROOM.

judge, clerk, bailiff, attorneys, etc., unless invited to cross. This invitation occurs when your case is called by the clerk. At this point you come forward and sit at the long table (known as the counsel table) just inside the fence. You and your witnesses sit facing the judge with your backs to the rest of the courtroom. In most Small Claims Courts, you will have been sworn (or affirmed if you wish) to tell the truth before the judge arrives. If this has not already been done, the oath will be administered at this time. In the great majority of Small Claims Courts you, your opponent and your witnesses will present the entire case from the long table. This means that you do not sit in the witness box next to the judge. Many people feel that it is polite to stand when addressing the judge, but you should do what feels most comfortable to you.

When your case is called and you come forward to take your

turn at the counsel table, have all your papers with you ready to present to the judge. This can include bills, receipts, estimates, photographs, contracts, letter to or from your opponent, etc. When the time comes to show these to the judge, you simply hand them to the clerk who will pass them on to the judge. As I have said before, documentation is a great aid to your case, but don't go overboard. Judges are a little like donkeys — load them too heavily and they are likely to lie down and go to sleep.

E. DEALING WITH YOUR OPPONENT

Before you get to the courtroom, you should do a little thinking about your opponent. Perhaps you can guess what sort of presentation he or she will make. If so, ask yourself how you can best deal with these arguments. This may be a good way to take the negative energy you may feel (frustration, annoyance, anger) and turn it into creative planning and preparation. In court, be polite. You will gain nothing, and may lose the respect of the judge, if you are obviously hostile or sarcastic. Don't interrupt your opponent when he or she is speaking — you will get your chance. When you present your case, lay out the facts to the judge; don't conduct an argument with the other side.

F. DEALING WITH THE JUDGE

It is hard to generalize about judges — each is an individual. I have seen more good than bad, but that doesn't help if your case comes up before an idiot. Unlike higher courts, no great intellectual ability is required to be a good Small Claims Court judge — indeed, most of the judges sitting on the United States Supreme Court would probably be lousy at it. What is required is a liking for people, openmindedness and, above all, patience. Everyone who comes to Small Claims Court should have the feeling that they got a fair chance to have their say.

Most Small Claims Court judges are judges in the more formal Municipal Courts who also hear the Small Claims calendar. This is a mistake. The last thing that is needed in Small Claims Court is the "me judge, you peasant" philosophy of our formal court system. Hopefully as Small Claims Court expands in the future, it will be staffed by people (not necessarily lawyers) specifically trained to meet its needs (see Chapter 24).

In California and many other states, lawyers are often appointed as temporary judges when a judge is ill or on vacation. The legal slang for a temporary judge is "Judge, pro tem". If your case comes up on a day when there is a "Judge, pro tem", you have one small advantage: you can choose whether or not to have your case heard by that particular person. How does this work? Under the law you are not required to have your case heard by a "pro tem" judge — you can ask that the hearing be delayed until a regular judge is available. Simply sit and watch the cases that are heard before yours. If the judge seems OK to you, go ahead when your turn comes. But, if for some reason you don't like the "pro tem" judge, ask that your case be delayed until another day. You don't have to state a reason — this is your right.

When thinking about presenting your case to a judge, there is one constructive thing that you can do. Imagine yourself in the judge's shoes. What would you value most from the people appearing before you? Before I ever sat as a judge, my answer was politeness, good organization of the material to be presented and reasonable brevity. After experiencing Small Claims Court from the judge's chair, I would only add — documented evidence. By this, I mean evidence that is supported by more than the word of the person bringing, or defending, the case. Witnesses, written statements, police accident reports, photographs — all these give the judge a chance to make a decision on something more than who tells the best story. And one final thing. Remember, the judge has heard thousands of stories very much like yours and will either cease paying attention or get annoyed if you try repeating your story three times.

14

WITNESSES

It is often helpful to have someone in court with you who has a first hand knowledge of the facts of your case and who can support your point of view. In many types of cases, such as car accidents, or disputes concerning whether or not a tenant left an apartment clean, witnesses are particularly valuable. In other fact situations, they aren't as necessary. For example, if a friend borrowed $500 and didn't pay it back, you don't need a witness to prove that your friend's (ex-friend's?) signature on the promissory note is genuine unless you expect him to base his defense on the theory that his signature was forged.

To arrange for a witness, simply talk to people you believe have something helpful to say and see if they will come down to the court and say it. You should do this even though subpoena forms are available from the Small Claims clerk's office to require a person's presence (see A below for details). Subpoenas are helpful when a person would otherwise have difficulty getting off work or school, but should almost never be used to drag someone in who doesn't want to come. Courts have lists of interpreters available if there is a language difficulty, but you should contact them well in advance if an interpreter will be needed.

A good witness should have first hand knowledge of the facts in dispute. This means that he or she saw the car accident, or the dog bite, or the dirty apartment, etc. The judge will not be interested in the testimony of a person who is repeating second hand or generalized information such as "I know Joe is a good, safe driver and would never have done anything reckless," or "I didn't see Joe's apartment before he moved out, but both Joe and his mother, who couldn't be here today, told me that they worked for two days cleaning it up."

A good witness is believable. This isn't always a quality of easy definition — a policeman may be a symbol of honesty to some people, while others regard him or her with hostility and fear. But remember, it is the judge you are trying to convince and judges tend to be fairly establishment folk (they make comfortable salaries, own their own homes and generally tend to like the existing order of things). Most judges I know would tend to believe a policeman.

In many types of cases such as a car accident, you won't have much choice as to witnesses. You will be lucky to have one. But in other disputes (was the house properly painted, or the work on the car engine completed?), you have an opportunity to plan ahead. When you do, try to get a witness who is particularly knowledgeable about the dispute in question. Thus, in a dispute over whether car repairs were properly done, bring a working car mechanic rather than your neighbor "who knows a lot about cars". Close friends and family are often your only witnesses. There is no rule that says that you can't have these people testify for you. Indeed, I have often seen a person's spouse, or the friend that he/she lives with, give very convincing testimony. But, given a choice, it is better to have a witness who is not your close friend or kin. A judge may discount testimony of people to whom you are close on the theory that they would naturally be biased in your favor.

I will talk more about witnesses as I go through the various case examples (Chapters 16-21), but let's outline a few basic do's and don'ts here:

☆ Never bring a witness to court who is hostile to you or hostile to the idea of testifying;

☆ Never bring a witness to court unless you know exactly what he or she will say. This sounds basic, but I have seen people lose cases because their witnesses supported the other side or got mixed up;

☆ Never pay, or offer to pay, a witness. It is a crime to do so. A subpoenaed witness is entitled to a small witness fee (see A below), but no other money;

☆ Never use a subpoena form to require a witness to be present unless you have made sure that it is OK with the witness (more in A below);

Prepare your witness thoroughly as to what your position is, what your opponent is likely to say and what you want the witness to say. In court, the witness will be on his/her own and you want to be sure that the story comes out right. It is completely legal to thoroughly discuss the case with the witness before hand.

IMPORTANT: In court a witness will be pretty much on his or her own. The witness will sit with you at the table facing the judge. Normally a witness doesn't take the witness stand in Small Claims. Most judges prefer that you don't pretend to be a lawyer and ask the witness a lot of questions. Simply let the witness explain what happened as he or she saw it. The judge may ask the witness questions. If you feel that the witness has left something out, you should ask a question designed to produce the information that you want.

A. SUBPOENAING WITNESSES

In California and most other states, you can require that a witness be present if that person resides within 150 miles of the courthouse (the distance varies state-to-state). To do this, go to the clerk's office and get a "Subpoena" form. Fill it out, and have it served on the person who you wish to have present. But remember, you never want to subpoena a person unless you have talked to him/her first and gotten an OK. The very act of dragging someone into court who doesn't want to come may set him/her against you. A subpoenaed witness is entitled to a fee of $12.00 and 20¢ per mile. The person serving the subpoena must have this money ready to pay if it is requested. If you win your case, you will probably be able to recover your witness fees from the other side. The judge has discretion as to whether to grant you your witness fees. Some judges are strict about this, making the loser pay the winner's witness fees only if he or she finds that the subpoenaed witness was essential to the presentation of the case. This means that, if your case is so strong that you don't need a witness but you subpoena one anyway, you may well have to pay the witness fee even though you win the case.

Here is the standard California subpoena form. You will need to prepare an original and two copies. Once prepared, take the subpoena form to the Small Claims Court clerk who will issue it.

Service must be made personally and the "Proof of Service", which is on the back of the subpoena, returned to the clerk's office. Rules for service are discussed in Chapter 11.

B. SUBPOENAING POLICE OFFICERS

You have probably already noticed that on the subpoena form, there is a special box to use if you wish to subpoena a police officer. The box is easy to fill out, but hard to pay for. The deposit to subpoena a police officer is at least $75. This money must be paid to the clerk at the time the subpoena is issued. Depending on the amount of the officer's time that is used, you may eventually get a refund of some of your $75.

C. SUBPOENAING DOCUMENTS

In addition to witnesses, you can also subpoena documents. It is rare that this is done in Small Claims Court, but it may occasionally be helpful. Someone (police department, phone company, hospital, corporation) may have certain books, ledgers, papers or other documents that can help your case. To get them, you must prepare a form entitled "Subpoena Duces Tecum". This is very similar to the standard subpoena form, except that there is a space to describe the papers or other documents that you want brought to court. To get a "Subpoena Duces Tecum" issued, you must attach an affidavit stating why you need the written material. Prepare three copies of all papers and, after you get the clerk to issue the subpoena, serve it on the witness using personal service as described in Chapter 11. As with a regular subpoena, the witness is entitled to ask for a $12.00 witness fee plus mileage. The "Proof of Service" is on the back of the subpoena form and must be filled out and returned to the clerk.

A Subpoena Duces Tecum must be directed to the person who is in charge of the documents, books or records that you want. It may take you a few phone calls to find out who this is. Be sure you get this information accurately. If you list someone on the "Subpoena Duces Tecum" who has nothing to do with the documents, you won't get them. When dealing with a large corporation, public utility, municipal government, etc., it is wise to list the person who is in overall charge of the department where the records are kept. Thus, if you want records from a public library having to do with library fines, or from the city tax and license department having to do with business license fees, you should not list the city manager or the mayor, but should list the head librarian or the director of the tax and license office.

EXAMPLE: Let's take a hypothetical case. You are being sued by the city on behalf of the public library for $300 for eight rare books which they state you failed to return. You know that you did return the books, but can't seem to get that across to the library which insists on treating you like a thief. You learn that each April the library takes a yearly inventory of all books on their shelves. You believe that, if you can get access to that inventory, you may be able to figure out where the library misplaced the books. Your first step is to ask the library to voluntarily open the inventory to you. If they refuse, you may well want to subpoena them. Here's how to do it:

Name, address and telephone no of attorney(s)

This space for court clerk only

John O'Gara
15 Scenic St.
Los Angeles, CA. 90011

Attorney(s) for   IN PRO PER

MUNICIPAL COURT OF CALIFORNIA, COUNTY OF LOS ANGELES

JUDICIAL DISTRICT

Public Library
                    Plaintiff(s) vs

John O'Gara
                    Defendant(s)
        (Abbreviated Title)

CASE NUMBER
(Fill in number)

SUBPENA DUCES TECUM
(Civil)

THE PEOPLE OF THE STATE OF CALIFORNIA, to   Robert Ringle, Head Librarian

You are ordered to appear in this court, located at

(Street Address of Court and City)

on   at   m.,   (Department, Division or Room No if any)   , to testify as a witness in this action
        (Date)   (Time)

You must appear at that time unless you make a special agreement to appear at another time, etc., with:

John O'Gara   at   584-1921
(Name of Attorney or Party Requesting This Subpena Duces Tecum)   (Telephone Number)

You are also ordered to bring with you the books, papers and documents or other things in your possession or under your control, described in the attached declaration or affidavit as follows: (Type or Print)

All book inventory information collected by the main branch of the Public Library during the calendar year 19__ which is more particularly described in the attached declaration.

Disobedience of this subpena may be punished as contempt by this court. You will also be liable for the sum of one hundred dollars and all damages to such party resulting from your failure to attend or to bring the books, etc., described above.

(To be completed when subpena is directed to a California highway patrolman, sheriff, marshal or policeman, etc.)
This subpena is directed to a member of
                                                    (Name of Employing Agency)
I certify that the fees required by law are deposited with this court:
    Receipt No.:   Amount Deposited $

Dated   , Clerk

(SEAL)   By   , Deputy

Note The original declaration or affidavit must be filed with the court clerk and a copy served with this subpena duces tecum

(See reverse side for Proof of Service)

Form Approved by the
Judicial Council of California
Effective Nov 10, 1969

SUBPENA DUCES TECUM (Civil)

CCP §§ 1985-1997, Evid C §§ 1560
1566, Gov C §§ 68097 1 68097 4, etc

78SB09L—C: 30 (9)— Cdb 8-74

1. Fill in the box on the form where you are asked to describe the books and records you want as follows: "All book inventory information collected by the main branch of the public library during the calendar year 19____ more particularly described in the attached declaration."

2. Prepare your declaration. It should be brief. There is no pre-printed form for this. Get a piece of 8½ x 11" legal paper from a stationery store (the kind with numbers on the side). Type the heading just as it appears on the subpoena form. Then identify the documents that you want brought to court and why you want them. Don't argue the merits of your case.

1	JOHN O'GARA
2	15 Scenic Street Los Angeles, California
3	849-1921
4	IN PROPRIA PERSONA
5	
6	SMALL CLAIMS COURT OF CALIFORNIA, COUNTY OF LOS ANGELES
7	LOS ANGELES JUDICIAL DISTRICT
8	

9	Public Library, Plaintiff)	Case Number ___(fill-in)___
10	vs.)	DECLARATION OF JOHN O'GARA
11	John O'Gara, Defendant)	
12	)	

13 I, John O'Gara, hereby declare that during the spring of 1979 I returned

14 six books to the Public Library. On July 1, 19__, the Public Library sued me

15 for the value of these books, claiming that I hadn't returned them. On July 5,

16 19__ I asked to see any and all book inventory records that the library main-

17 tained. I learned that during the week of May 20, 19__ an inventory had been

18 taken (this was after I returned the books), but I was told that it was not a

19 public document and that it would take too long to go through it to see if

20 the books that are the subject of this dispute had been misplaced. I believe

21 that, if I can get access to the library inventory, I can show that the books

22 were returned.

23 This declaration is made under penalty of perjury at ___Los Angeles___
                                                              City

24 California on ____July 15, 19____ .
                        Date

25

26   _____
                                        (signature)

27   JOHN O'GARA

28   (Notarization is not necessary)

116

3. Staple your declaration to the Subpoena Duces Tecum form and have the subpoena issued by the Small Claims clerk. Then have the subpoena served, being sure that the "Proof of Service" (see Chapter 11 F) is properly filled out and returned to the clerk.

NOTE: On the day of the hearing the person who you have subpoenaed will show up with the documents in question. The documents will be presented to the court — not you. If you need an opportunity to examine the documents, request it from the judge. He or she may well let you do your examining right there in the courtroom while other cases go ahead, or, if necessary, he may continue the case for a few days and arrange to have you make your examination at the place of business of the owner of the records.

D. JUDGES AS WITNESSES

California Code of Civil Procedure Section 117 states, "The Judge may consult witnesses informally and otherwise investigate the controversy." In practice this means as much, or as little, as an individual judge wants it to mean. But it clearly does allow the conscientious judge great discretion to climb down off the bench to check out an important fact.

Using a judge as a witness is a valuable technique in many situations. This is done routinely in many types of disputes, such as clothing cases in which you bring the damaged garment into court for the judge's examination. As I have said repeatedly in this book, always bring into court any physical evidence that will help your case and fit through the door.

But what if your evidence won't fit through the door (a car with a poor paint job) or can't be brought into the building (a supposedly pedigreed puppy that grew up looking as if Lassie were the mother and Rin Tin Tin the father)? Why not ask the judge to accompany you outside the building to examine the car, or the dog, or whatever else is important to your case? Many (but not all) judges are willing to do so if they feel that it is necessary to a better understanding of the case and won't take too long. But never ask a judge to take time to leave his or her court to view evidence if you can prove your case just as well by other means, such as witnesses and pictures. A good approach is to do as well as you can in court, and to ask the judge to view evidence outside of court only if it is essential.

E. TESTIMONY BY TELEPHONE

A Small Claims Court judge has the power to take testimony or otherwise investigate a case over the phone. Many judges don't like to do this, but a number will if a witness cannot be present because he or she is ill, disabled, out-of-state, or can't take off from work. While procedures vary, some courts will set up conference calls so that the opposing party has the opportunity to hear what is being said and to respond.

Don't just assume that a particular judge will allow information to be presented over the phone. Ask the clerk. If you get a negative response, don't give up — ask the judge when you get into the courtroom. It is also an extremely good idea to have a letter from the witness who you want to reach by phone, explaining what he or she will testify to (e.g., your opponent's car ran a red light and broadsided you) and explaining why it is impossible for him or her to be in court. Such a letter might look like this.

---

37 Ogden Court
Ukiah, CA

Presiding Judge
Small Claims Court
Ukiah, California

September 30, 19--

Re: John Swift vs.
     Peter Patrakos
     Case # 11478

Your Honor:

On September 15, 19--, I witnessed an auto accident at the corner of Hennepin and Eighth in Ukiah, involving John Swift and Peter Patrakos. I clearly saw Mr. Patrokos' car, which was heading north on South Dora, go through a red light and hit Mr. Swift's blue van which was proceeding south on West 7th, well inside the 30 MPH speed limit.

Mr. Swift has asked me to testify on his behalf, and normally I would be happy to do so. However, I will be in New York City on business during the months of October, November and December 19-- and cannot be present.

I have asked Mr. Swift to let me know the day and approximate time of the court hearing and have told him that I will give him a phone number where I can be reached. If you think it desireable, I will be pleased to give my testimony by phone.

Sincerely,

Victor Van Cleve

15

PRESENTING YOUR CASE TO THE JUDGE

A. UNCONTESTED CASES — GETTING A JUDGMENT BY DEFAULT

Surprisingly often, presenting your case will be easy — your opponent will simply not show up. If this occurs, you will not have to make a formal presentation of your entire case. The judge will check to see that your opponent was properly served and may ask you a question or two to make sure that there is no obvious flaw in your case such as the Statute of Limitations having run out two years ago. He or she will also ask you to present the basic facts of your case briefly, but will not want a long argument or lots of evidence.* It's as if you were scheduled to play a ballgame and the other team failed to show up. You win by default — you don't need to hit the ball over the fence and run around the bases. And there is no appeal from a default judgment. If a defendant doesn't show up to argue his case, he can't appeal to the appellate division of the Superior Court (see Chapter 22).

Very occasionally a person who has defaulted will show up in court a few days later with a super excuse. The judge does have the discretion to set aside a default in this situation and re-open

_____
* C.C.P. Section 117(a).

the case. This is rarely done and in no case will it be done if the defaulting party delays in requesting that the judgment be set aside. For example, if the defaulting party shows up three weeks after a default judgment was entered to request that it be set aside, he would have the burden of explaining to the judge why he didn't show up or phone earlier. As you might guess, not many people can lift a burden this heavy. (We discuss the mechanics of setting aside a default in Chapter 10 E). In almost all situations, motions to set aside defaults *must* be made within 30 days after the default was entered.

B. CONTESTED CASES

Assuming now that both sides show up and step forward when the case is called by the clerk, what happens next? First, the judge will establish everyone's identity. Next, he will ask the plaintiff to briefly state his case.

The plaintiff should tell the judge what is in dispute and then briefly outline his position. It is critical that the judge know what the case is about before you start arguing it. For example, if your case involves a car accident, you might start by saying, "This case involves a car accident at Cedar and Rose Streets in which my car suffered $372 worth of damage", not "It all started when I was driving down Rose Street after having two eggs and a danish for breakfast." Only occasionally have I seen a case where the plaintiff's initial presentation should take longer than five minutes. As part of his or her statement the plaintiff should present any papers, photos or other documentary evidence. These should be handed to the clerk and explained. The plaintiff should also be sure to indicate the presence of any witnesses to the judge.

When the plaintiff is finished, the judge may wish to ask questions. He or she may or may not wish to hear from the plaintiff's witnesses before the defendant speaks. Each judge will control the flow of evidence differently. It's best to go with the judge's energy, not against it. Just be sure that, at one time or another, you have made all of your points. If you feel rushed, say so. The judge will normally slow things down a little.

Sooner or later the defendant will get his chance. Defendants often get so angry at something the plaintiff has said ("lies! lies!")

that when their turn comes, they immediately attack. This is silly and usually counter-productive. The defendant should calmly and clearly present his side of the dispute to the judge. If the plaintiff has made false or misleading statements, these should be answered, but at the end of the presentation, not the beginning. Tell your story first, then deal with the plaintiff's testimony if this seems necessary.

Here are a few tips that you may find helpful. These are not rules written on golden tablets, but only suggestions. You may want to follow some and ignore others.

1. Stand when you make your initial presentation to the judge. Standing gives most people a sense of presence and confidence at a time when they may be a little nervous. But this doesn't mean that you have to jump to your feet every time the judge asks you a question.

2. Don't read your statement. Reading in court is almost always a bore. Some people find it helpful to make a few notes on a card to serve as a reminder if they get nervous or forget something. If you decide to do this, list the headings of the various points you want to make in an outline form. Be sure your list is easy to read at a glance and that the topics are in the correct order.

3. Be brief.

4. Never interrupt your opponent or any of the witnesses no matter how outrageous their "lies". You will get your chance to respond.

5. Be prepared to present any section of your case that is difficult to get across in words, in another way. This means bringing your used car parts, damaged clothing or other exhibits, such as photographs or cancelled checks with you, and having them organized for easy presentation.

6. There will be a blackboard in court. If a drawing would be helpful, as they almost always are in cases involving car accidents, be sure that you have practiced at home. You will want to draw clearly and legibly the first time. If you wish to make a drawing and the judge doesn't ask you to, simply request permission to do so.

A SAMPLE CONTESTED CASE: Now let's take a typical case and pretend that a court reporter is present making a transcript.

Clerk: "The next case is John Andrews v. Robertson Realty. Will everyone please come forward?" (Four people come forward and sit at the table facing the judge.)

Judge: "Good morning. Which one of you is Mr. Andrews? OK, will you begin, Mr. Andrews?"

John Andrews: (stands) "This is a case about my failure to get a $400 cleaning deposit returned, your Honor. I rented a house from Robertson Realty at 1611 Spruce St. in Fresno in March of 198_, on a month-to-month tenancy. On January 10, 198_, I sent Mr. Robertson a written notice that I was planning to move on March 10. In fact, I moved out on March 8 and left the place extremely clean. All of my rent was properly paid. A few days after I moved out, I asked Mr. Robertson to return my $400 deposit. He refused, saying that the place was dirty and that he was keeping my deposit.

I have with me a copy of a letter I wrote to Mr. Robertson on March 15 setting out my position in more detail. I also have some photographs that my friend Carol Spann, who is here as a witness, took on the day I moved out. I believe the pictures show pretty clearly that I did a thorough clean-up. (John Andrews hands the letter and pictures to the clerk who hands them to the judge.)

Your Honor, I am asking not only for the $400 deposit, but also for $200 in punitive damages that the law allows a tenant when a landlord improperly refuses to return a deposit." *

Judge: "Mr. Andrews, will you introduce your witness."

Andrews: "Yes, this is Carol Spann. She helped me clean up and move on March 7 and 8"

Judge: (Looking at the pictures) "Ms. Spann, were you in the apartment the day John Andrews moved out?"

Carol Spann: (standing) "Yes, I was and the day before too. I helped clean up and I can say that we did a good job. Not only did we do the normal washing and scrubbing, but we waxed the kitchen floor and shampooed the rugs."

Judge: (turning to Mr. Robertson) "OK, now it's your turn to tell me why the deposit wasn't returned."

Harry Robertson: (standing) "I don't know how they could have cleaned the place up, your Honor, because it was filthy when I inspected it on March 9. Let me give you a few specifics. There was mildew and mold around the bathtub, the windows were filthy, the refrigerator hadn't been defrosted and there was dog — how shall I say it — dog manure in the basement. Your Honor, I have brought along Clem Houndstooth as a witness. Mr. Houndstooth is the tenant who moved in three days after Mr. Andrews moved out. Incidentally, your Honor, the place was so dirty that I only charged Mr. Houndstooth a $200 cleaning deposit, because he agreed to clean it up himself."

Judge: (looking at Clem Houndstooth) "Do you wish to say something?"

Clem Houndstooth: (standing) "Yes, I do. Mr. Robertson asked me to

* The legal rules on returning deposits and punitive damages are contained in Section 1950.5 of the California Civil Code and are more particularly described in Chapter 8 of *The California Tenants' Handbook*, Moskovitz, Warner and Sherman, Nolo Press (see back of this book for order information).

come down and back him up and I am glad to do it because I put in two full days cleaning that place up. I like a clean house, your Honor, not a half-way clean, half-way dirty house. I just don't think a house is clean if the oven is full of gunk, there is mold in the bathroom, and the insides of the cupboards are grimy. All these conditions existed at 1611 Spruce St. when I moved in. I just don't believe that anyone could think that that place was clean."

Judge: "Mr. Andrews, do you have anything to add?"

John Andrews: (standing up) "Yes, I sure do. First, as to the mildew problem. The house is forty years old and there is some dampness in the wall of the bathroom. Maybe there is a leaky pipe someplace behind the tile. I cleaned it a number of times, but it always came back. I talked to Mr. Fisk in Mr. Robertson's office about the problem about a month after I moved in he told me that I would have to do the best I could because they couldn't afford to tear the wall apart. As to the cupboards and stove, they are both old. The cabinets haven't been painted in ten years, so, of course, they aren't perfect, and that old stove was a lot dirtier when I moved in than it is now."

Judge: "What about the refrigerator, Mr. Andrews? Was that defrosted?"

John Andrews: "No, your Honor, it wasn't, but it had been defrosted about three weeks before I moved out and I thought that it was good enough the way it was."

Judge: "OK, if no one else has anything to add, I want to return your pictures and letters. You will receive my decision by mail in a few days."

Now, I have a little surprise for you. This was a real case taking place not in Fresno in 198_, but in Small Claims Court in San Francisco on September 14, 1977. As they used to say on Dragnet, "Only the names have been changed to protect the innocent." And I have another surprise for you. I spoke to the judge after the court session and I know how the case came out. The judge explained his reasoning to me as follows.

"This is a typical case in which both sides have some right on their side. What is clean to one person may be dirty to another. Based on what I heard, I would have to guess that the old tenant made a fairly conscientious effort to clean up and probably left the place about as clean as it was when he moved in, but that the new tenant, Houndstooth, had much higher standards and convinced the landlord that it was filthy. The landlord may not have needed too much convincing since he probably would just as well keep the deposit. But I did hear enough to convince me that Andrews, the old tenant, didn't do a perfect job cleaning up. My decision will be that Andrews gets a judgment for the return of $250 of the $400 deposit, with no punitive damages. I believe that $150 is more than enough to compensate the landlord for any damages he suffered."

I then asked the judge if he felt that the case was well presented. He replied substantially as follows:

"Better than average. I think I got a pretty good idea of what the problems were. The witnesses were helpful and the pictures gave me an idea that the place wasn't a total mess. Both sides could have done better, however. Andrews could have had a witness to talk about the condition when he moved in if it was truly dirtier than when he left. Another witness to testify to the apartment's cleanliness when he moved out would have been good too. His friend, Carol Spann, seemed to be a very close friend and I wasn't sure that she was objective when it came to judging whether the place was clean. The landlord, Robertson, could also have done better. He could have presented a more disinterested witness, although I must say that Houndstooth's testimony was pretty convincing. Also he could have had pictures documenting the dirty conditions and an estimate from a cleaning company for how much they would have charged to clean the mess up. Without going to too much trouble, I think that either side could have probably done somewhat better with more thorough preparation."

C. DON'T FORGET TO ASK FOR YOUR COSTS

When you finish your presentation to the judge, you should be sure he realizes that you have incurred certain court costs. These can be added to the judgment amount. As we have mentioned, you can't recover for such things as time off from work, paying a babysitter or xerox charges. You can recover for:

✿ Your filing fee

✿ Service of process

✿ Subpoenaed witness fees

✿ Cost of necessary documents, such as verification of car ownership by the D.M.V.

If you forget to get your costs added to the judgment in court and want to go to the trouble, you can file a "Memorandum of Costs" with the Small Claims clerk within five days after judgment. Forms are available at the clerk's office. For information on recovering costs incurred after judgment when your opponent won't voluntarily pay the judgment, see Chapter 24 C.

16

MOTOR VEHICLE REPAIR CASES

Most Small Claims Court cases fall into a dozen or so broad categories with perhaps another dozen sub-categories. In the next six chapters, we look at the most common types of cases and discuss strategies to handle each. Even if your fact situation doesn't fit neatly in one of these categories, read them all. By taking a few hints here and a little information there, you should be able to piece together a good plan of action. For example, suggestions I make to handle motor vehicle repair disputes can easily be applied to cases involving major appliances such as televisions, washers, expensive stereos, etc.

Let's start by imagining that you go to the auto repair shop to pick up your trusty, but slightly greying, steed. The bill is $725 for a complete engine overhaul. This seems a little steep, but after the mechanic tells you all about the great job he did, and you remember that inflation is a fact of life, you drive out of the garage in something approaching a cheerful mood. One of life's little hassles has been taken care of, at least temporarily.

You're right — temporarily can sometimes be a very short time. In this case, it lasts only until you head up the first hill. What's that funny noise, you think? Why don't I have more power? Oh shit, you say (you never swear, but there are some extreme provocations where nothing else will do). You turn around and drive back to the garage. Not only are you out $725, but your car works worse than it did when you brought it in.

Funny, no one seems as pleasant as they did before. Funny, no one seems to have time to listen to you. Finally, after several explanations and a bit of foot stomping, you get someone to say that they will look the car over again. You take a bus home, trying not to be paranoid. Two days later, you call. Nothing has been done. You yell at the garage owner and then call your bank to stop payment on the check. You are told that they cashed it yesterday. Another few days pass and the garage tells you that the problem is in a part of the engine that they didn't work on. You only paid for a "short block job" they keep telling you. "Give us another $300 and we can surely solve this new problem," they add.

In disgust, you go down and pick up your crippled friend and drive it home — very, very slowly. You are furious and decide to pursue every legal remedy, no matter what the trouble. How do you start?

First, park your car, take a shower and have a glass of wine. Nothing gets decided well when you're mad. Now, going back to the reasoning we used at the beginning of this book, ask yourself some basic questions:

A. HAVE I SUFFERED A LOSS?

That's easy. Your car doesn't work, you paid out a lot of money and the garage wants another bundle to fix it. Clearly, you have suffered a loss.

B. DID THE NEGLIGENCE OF THE GARAGE CAUSE MY LOSS?

Ah ha, now we get to the nitty gritty. In this type of case you can almost always expect the garage to claim that they did their work properly and that the car simply needs more work. Maybe the garage is right — it's your job to prove that they aren't. Doing so will make your case; failing to do so will break it. You better get to work.

Step 1 Collect Available Evidence

First, get all evidence together where time is of the essence. In this fact situation, this means getting your used parts (it's a good idea to do this anytime you have major work done).* If the garage will not give them to you, make your request by letter, keeping a copy for your file. If you get the parts, fine — if you don't, you have evidence that the garage is badly run or has something to hide.

Step 2 Have The Car Checked

Before you drive many miles, have your car checked by an established local mechanic or mechanics. Often it is possible to get free estimates from repair shops. But be sure that at least one of the people who looks the car over is willing to come with you to Small Claims Court it the need arises.

Step 3 Try To Settle Your Case

By now you should have a pretty good idea as to what the first garage did wrong. Call them and ask that either the job be re-done, or that they give you a refund of part or all of your money. Often the repair shop will agree to do some, or all, of the work over to avoid a further hassle. If they do agree to take the car back, try to get a written agreement detailing what they will do and how long it will take. Also, talk to the mechanic who will actually work on the car to be sure he understands what needs to be done.

Step 4 Write A Demand Letter

If the garage isn't cooperative, it's time to write them a formal demand letter. Remember our discussion in Chapter 6. Your letter should be short, polite and written with an eye to a judge reading it. In this situation you could write something like this:

NOTE: Most small independent garages don't make any written warranty or guaranty of their work. However, if you were given any promises in writing, mention them here in your letter.

---

* In California you are entitled to get your parts back by law, just as you are entitled to a written estimate before repairs are made. See the *Compleat California Consumer Catalogue,* available from the California Department of Consumer Affairs, 1020 N St., Sacramento, Calif. 95814.

```
                              Haig Mackey
                              15 Orange St.
                              Laguna Beach, CA

     Happy Days Motors
     100 Speedway
     Corona Del Mar, CA

     Dear People:

        On August 13, 198-, I brought my 1972 Dodge to your garage.  You
     agreed to do a complete engine rebuild job for $725.  You told me,
     "Your car will be running like a watch when we're through with it."
     The car worked well when I brought it in, but was a little short on
     power.  Two days later when I picked up my car, it barely moved at
     all.  The engine made such a clanging noise that I have been afraid
     to drive it.

        I have repeatedly asked you to fix the car or to refund my money.
     You have refused.  Shortly after the work was done, I also asked for
     my used parts to be returned.  You refused to give them to me even
     though this is a violation of state law.

        I have had several mechanics look my car over since you worked
     on it.  They all agree that you did your job improperly and even
     installed some used parts that came from a 1974 Plymouth.  The
     work you did on the engine rings was particularly badly done.

        After receiving no response from you, I had the work re-done at a
     cost of $610.  My car now works well.  Please refund my $725.  Should
     you fail to do so, I will exhaust all my legal remedies including
     complaining to interested state and local agencies and taking this
     dispute to Small Claims Court.

        May I hear from you promptly.

                              Haig  Mackey


     cc:  California Dept. of Consumer Affairs
          Bureau of Automotive Repair
          3116 Bradshaw Road
          Sacramento, CA
```

Step 5 File Your Court Papers

If you still get no satisfactory response from the garage, file
your papers at the Small Claims clerk's office of your local Small
Claims Court. Re-read Chapters 7–10.

Step 6 Prepare For Court

If you want a third person (a judge) to understand your case,
you must understand it yourself. Sounds simple, doesn't it? It
does to me too until I get involved with machinery. My opinion of
cars (and most other machinery) is low — they are supposed to
work without trouble, but most of us know better.

For me to argue a case in Small Claims such as the one we are talking about here could be a disaster unless I did some homework. This sort of disaster is repeated often in Small Claims. I have seen many, many people argue cases about their cars knowing no more than "the car was supposed to be fixed, your Honor, and it's worse than ever". On some mornings when the roses are in bloom, the peaches are sweet and the angels are in heaven, this is enough to win — usually it isn't. Why? Because the people from the garage are likely to have a terrific sounding story about the wonderful job they did. They will talk about pistons, rings, bearings, pulling the head and turning the cam shaft. It's all likely to sound so impressive that you can easily find yourself on the defensive.

This sort of thing needn't happen if you are willing to learn a little about your car (or whatever machinery is involved). Fifteen minutes' conversation with a knowledgeable mechanic may be all you need to understand what's going on. Also, your local library will have manuals about every type of car, complete with diagrams, etc.

REMEMBER THE JUDGE: In Chapter 13 I mentioned that it's important to pay attention to whom you are presenting your case. Most Small Claims judges don't understand the insides of cars any better than you do. People often become lawyers because they don't like to get their hands dirty. So be prepared to deal with a person who nods his head but doesn't really understand the difference between the drive shaft and the axle. Car cases are often easier to present to a woman judge. Women don't usually have the same ego involvement with cars that men do. They are more willing to say "I don't know".

Step 7 Appearing In Court

When you appear in court, be sure that you are well organized. Bring all the letters you have written, or received, about your car problem as well as written warranties (if any), photographs if they are helpful and your used parts if they aid in making your case. Several times in cases involving machinery, I have seen people give effective testimony by presenting a large drawing illustrating the screw-up. Also, be sure that you get your witnesses to the courtroom on time. The best way to do this is to pick them up at home or work and personally escort them.

If you are well prepared you should win the sort of case outlined here without difficulty. Judges drive cars and have to get them fixed; they tend to be sympathetic with this type of consumer complaint. Simply present your story (see Chapter 15), your documentation and your witnesses. If you feel that your opponent is snowing the judge with a lot of technical lingo, get his (her) Honor back on the track by asking that the technical terms be explained in ordinary English. This will be a relief to everyone in the courtroom except your opponent. You will likely find that, once his case is shorn of all the magic words, it will shrink from tiger to pussycat.

17

MOTOR VEHICLE
PURCHASE CASES

All too often someone buys a motor vehicle, drives it a short way, and watches it fall apart. All too often the seller won't stand behind the product sold or work out some sort of fair adjustment. There are major differences in approach between buying a new vehicle from a dealer, buying a used vehicle from a dealer and buying a used vehicle from a private party. Let's look at each situation individually:

A. NEW VEHICLES *

Here the most common problem is the lemon with major manufacturing defects that the dealer won't fix under the new vehicle warranty. These sorts of cases are often won by irate consumers, but winning is no sure thing. The dealers have all been sued before; they know what to say and how to say it. Defending lawsuits is part of their business. Success will depend on your preparing your case carefully. Your goal is to prove that the vehicle was defective or latently defective when purchased, and that

---

* Several automobile companies also offer binding arbitration as an alternative. In the Bay Area, arbitration is available for General Motors and Volkswagen-Porsche-Audi cars through the Better Business Bureau, 2740 Van Ness, San Francisco, CA 94109. Ford also has their own program, but most people familiar with it feel that it is best avoided.

the defect should have been fixed under the warranty. You also need to prove the amount of money you are out as a result of the problem. You may also have to deal with a dealer's claim that the defect was caused by your improper use of the vehicle.

Commonly problems develop with new vehicles just at the time the warranty runs out. Sometimes it seems as though there is a little destruct switch set to flip fifteen minutes after you hit "one year or ten thousand miles, whichever comes first". Often too, a problem starts to surface while the car is still under warranty and a dealer makes inadequate repairs which last scarcely longer than the remainder of the warranty term. When the same problem develops again after the warranty has run out, the dealer refuses to fix it.

Just the other day I saw a case involving this sort of problem. A man with a new, expensive European car sued the local dealer and the parent car company's West Coast representative. He claimed that he had repeatedly brought the car into the dealer's repair shop with transmission problems while it was still under warranty. Each time adjustments were made which seemed to eliminate the problem. But each time, after a month or so, the same problem would reappear. A few months after the warranty ran out, the transmission died. Even though the car was only a little over a year old, and had gone less than 10,000 miles, both the dealer and the parent car company refused to repair it. Their refusals continued even though the owner repeatedly wrote them, demanding action.

How did the car owner go about dealing with his problem? First, because he needed his car, he went ahead and had the repairs made. This involved a cost in excess of $750. Then, he filed his Small Claims action. Because the dealer was located in the same city as he was, the man could sue locally.* In this situation it would have been adequate to sue only the local dealer and not the West Coast representative of the car company, but it didn't hurt to sue both following the general rule, "when in doubt, sue all possible defendants".

In court, the car owner was well prepared and had a reasonably easy time. Both he and his wife testified as to their trials and tribulations with the car. They gave the judge copies of the several letters they had written the dealer, one of which listed by

---

* Only one defendant need be local to sue in a particular judicial district. The fact that the car company's West Coast headquarters was in a different part of the state didn't cause a problem with bringing the suit where the dealer was located (see Chapter 9).

date the fifteen times they had taken the car to the dealer's shop. They also produced a letter from the owner of the independent garage which finally fixed the transmission stating that, when he took the transmission apart, he discovered a defect in its original assembly. The new car dealer simply testified that his mechanics had done their best to fix the car under the warranty. He then pointed out that, once the warranty had run out, he was no longer responsible. The dealer made no effort to challenge the car owner's story, nor did he bring his own mechanics to testify as to what they had done while the car was still under warranty. The car owner won. He presented a convincing case to the point that the defect had never been fixed when it should have been under the warranty. The dealer did nothing to rebut it. As the judge noted to me after the hearing, a $12,000 car should come with a transmission that will last longer than 10,000 miles. The car owner would have had an even stronger case if he had brought the independent garage man to court, but the letters, along with his own testimony and that of his wife, were adequate in a situation where the dealer didn't put up much of a defense.

NOTE: In this sort of case it is very convincing to have documentation of all the trips you have made to the dealer's repair shop. You may be able to find copies of work orders you signed, or cancelled checks if you were charged. If you don't have this sort of record, sit down with a calendar and do your best to make an accurate list. Give the list to the judge in court. He will accept it as true unless the car dealer disputes it.

Even if your car is no longer covered by a written warranty when trouble develops, you may have a case. There are general common law concepts of warranty that give you protection over and above the actual written paper that comes with the vehicle. Thus, if the engine on your properly maintained car burns out after 25,000 miles, you will stand a good chance of recovering some money even though the written warranty has expired. Engines are simply supposed to last longer than 25,000 miles. You may also wish to consider other remedies in addition to Small Claims Court such as trying to enlist the help of state regulatory agencies.* One strategy of last resort if you don't have much equity in the car is to simply drive it to the dealer and leave it

---

* Again I recommend the *Compleat California Consumer Catalogue* published by the State of California.

there, refusing to make any more payments until it is fixed. This is an extreme remedy and should only be considered in an extreme situation. It does have the beauty of shifting the responsibility to take action, legal or otherwise, to the other side. If you do this, be sure to set forth in writing all the circumstances surrounding the mechanical deficiencies and your efforts to remedy the situation, and send a copy to both the car dealer and the bank or other financial institution that has the loan.

B. USED VEHICLE DEALERS

Recovering from used vehicle dealers can be tricky for several reasons. Unlike new vehicle dealers who are usually somewhat dependent upon their reputation in the community for honesty, used vehicle dealers commonly have no positive reputation to start with and survive by becoming experts at self-protection. Also (and don't underestimate this one), judges almost never buy used vehicles and therefore aren't normally as sympathetic to the problems used vehicle owners encounter. Chances are a judge has had a problem getting his (her) new car fixed under a warranty, but has never bought a ten year old Plymouth in "tip-top shape", only to have it die two blocks after leaving Honest Al's.

The principal self-protection device employed by used vehicle dealers is the "as is" designation in the written sales contract. The salesperson may promise the moon, but when you read the fine print of the contract, you will see it clearly stated that the seller takes absolutely no responsibility for the condition of the vehicle.

Time and again I have sat in court and heard hard luck stories like this:

"I bought the car for $1,200 two months ago. The man at 'Lucky Larry's' told me that it had a completely reconditioned engine and transmission. I drove the car less than 400 miles and it died. I mean really died — it didn't roll over and dig itself a hole, but it may as well have. I had it towed to an independent garage and they told me that, as far as they could see, no engine or transmission work had ever been done. They estimated that to put the car right would cost $800.* I got one more estimate which was even

---

* Of course, this claim would have to be scaled down to $750 to fit into Small Claims Court (see Chapter 4).

higher, so I borrowed the $800 and had the work done. I feel I really got took by Lucky Larry. I have with me the cancelled check for the $800 in repairs, plus the mechanic who did the work who can testify as to the condition of the car when he saw it."

Unfortunately, this plaintiff will probably lose. Why? Because going back to the sort of issues that we discussed in Chapter 2, he has proven only half of his case. He has shown his loss (he bought a $1,200 car that wasn't worth $1,200), but he has not dealt with the issue of the defendant's responsibility to make the loss good ("liability"). Almost surely the used car dealer will testify that he "had no way of knowing how long a ten-year old Plymouth would last and that, for this very reason, sold the car "as is". He will then show the judge a written contract that not only has the "as is" designation, but which will say someplace in the fine print that "this written contract is the entire agreement between the parties and that no oral statements or representations made by the dealer or any salesperson are part of the contract".

How can you fight this sort of cynical semi-fraud? It's difficult to do so after the fact. The time for self-protection is before you buy a vehicle when you can have it checked by an expert and can insist that any promises made by the salesperson as to the condition of the car or the availability of repairs, be put in writing. Of course, good advice such as this, after the damage has been done, "isn't worth more than a passle of warm spit" as former Vice-President John Nance Garner so graphically put it. If you have just been cheated on a used car deal, you want to know what, if anything, you can do now. Here are some suggestions.

1. If the car broke almost immediately after you took it out of the used car lot, you can file in Small Claims and argue that you were defrauded. Your theory is that, no matter what the written contract said, there was also an implied warranty that you purchased a car, not a junk heap. When the dealer produces his "as is" contract, argue that it is no defense to fraud.

2. You may want to consider having the car towed back to the lot and refusing to make future payments. This puts the burden on the bank or finance company to sue you, at which point you can defend on the basis of fraud. If you take this approach, be sure you have excellent documentation that the car was truly a lemon. Of course, you will probably have made some down pay-

ment, so even in this situation you may wish to initiate action in Small Claims Court.

3. Have your car checked over by someone who knows cars and who would be willing to testify if need be. If this person can find affirmative evidence that you were cheated, you will greatly improve your Small Claims case. They might, for example, find that the speedometer had been tampered with in violation of state law, or that a heavy grade of truck oil had been put in the crank case so that the car wouldn't belch smoke. Also, this is the sort of case where a Subpoena Duces Tecum (subpoena for documents) might be of help (see Chapter 13). You might wish to subpoena records the car dealer has pertaining to his purchase price of the car, or its condition when purchased. It might also be helpful to learn the name of the car's former owner with the idea of contacting him (her). With a little digging you may be able to develop information that will enable you to convince a judge that you have been defrauded.

4. Consider other remedies besides Small Claims Courts. These can include checking with your state Department of Consumer Affairs, or the local Department of Motor Vehicles to see if used car lots are regulated. In California and many other states, the Department of Motor Vehicles licenses used car dealers and can

be very helpful in getting disputes resolved, particularly where your complaint is one of many against the same dealer for similar practices. Also, contact your local District Attorney's office. Most now have a consumer fraud division which can be ot great help. If you can convince them that what happened to you smells rotten, or your complaint happens to be against someone they have already identified as a borderline criminal, they will likely call the used car dealer in for a chat. In theory, the D.A.'s only job is to bring a criminal action which will be of no direct aid in getting your money back, but in practice, negotiations often go on which can result in restitution. In plain words, this means that the car dealer will be told, "Look buddy, you're right on the edge of the law here (or maybe over the edge). If you clean up your act, which means taking care of all complaints against you and seeing that there are no more, we will close your file. If you don't, I suggest you hire a good lawyer because you're going to need one."

C. USED VEHICLES FROM PRIVATE PARTIES

Normally it is easier to win a case against a private party than it is a used vehicle dealer. This runs counter to both common sense and fairness, as a private party is likely to be more honest than a dealer. But fair or not, the fact is that a non-dealer is usually less sophisticated in self-protection than is a pro. Indeed, in most private party sales the seller does no more than sign over the title slip in exchange for the agreed upon price. No formal contract is signed that says the buyer takes the car "as is".

If trouble develops soon after you purchase the vehicle and you are out money for unexpected repairs, you may be able to recover. Again, the problem is usually not proving your loss, but convincing the judge that the seller of the vehicle is responsible ("liable") to make your loss good. To do this, you normally must prove that the seller represented the vehicle to be in better shape than in fact it was, and that you relied on these promises when you made the deal.

Recently, I watched Barbara, a twenty year old college student, succeed in proving just such a case. She sued John for $425, claiming that the B.M.W. motorcycle she purchased from him was in far worse shape than he had advertised. In court, she ably and convincingly outlined her conversations with John around the purchase of the motorcycle, testifying that he repeatedly told her that the cycle was "hardly used". She hadn't gotten any of his promises in writing, but she did a creative job of developing and presenting what evidence she had. This included:

---

14 Stockton St.
Corte Madera, Calif.

January 27, 19___

John Malinosky
321 South Zaporah
Albany, Calif.

Dear Mr. Malinosky:

This letter is a follow-up to our recent phone conversation in which you refused to discuss the fact that the 1975 B.M.W. motorcycle I purchased from you on January 15 is not in the "excellent condition" that you claimed.

To review: on January 12 I saw your ad for a motorcycle that was "almost new - hardly used - excellent condition" in the local flea market newspaper. I called you and you told me that the cycle was a terrific bargain and that you would never sell it except that you needed money for school. I told you that I didn't know much about machinery.

The next day you took me for a ride on the cycle. You told me specifically that:

1. The cycle had just been tuned up.
2. The cycle had been driven less than 10,000 miles.
3. The cycle had never been raced or used roughly.
4. That if anything went wrong with the cycle in the next month or two, you would see that it was fixed.

I didn't have the cycle more than a week when the brakes went out. When I had them checked, the mechanic told me that the carburetor also needed work (I confirmed this with another mechanic - see attached estimate). The mechanics also told me that the cycle had been driven at least 50,000 miles (perhaps a lot more) and that it needed a tune-up. In addition they showed me caked mud and scratches under the cycle which indicated to them that it had been driven extensively off the road in rough terrain and had probably been raced on dirt tracks.

The low mechanic's estimate to do the repairs was $425. Before having the work done, I called you to explain the situation and to give you a chance to arrange for the repairs to be made, or to make them yourself. You laughed at me and said, "Sister, do what you need to do - you're not getting dime one from me."

Again I respectfully request that you make good on the promises you made to me on January 15. I enclose a copy of the mechanic's bill for $425 along with several higher estimates that I received from other repair shops.

Sincerely,

Barbara Parker

A copy of her letter to John which clearly outlined her position.

Copies of repair bills (and estimates) dated within two weeks of her purchase of the cycle, the lowest of which came to $425.

A copy of John's newspaper ad which she answered. It read: "B.M.W. 500 c.c. 1975 model, almost new — hardly used — excellent condition — $750."

Finally Barbara presented the judge with this note from the mechanic who fixed the cycle.

```
To Whom It May Concern:

     It's hard for me to get off work but if you need me, please ask the
judge to delay the case a few days.  All I have to say is this: the
B.M.W. that Barbara Parker brought to me was in fair shape.  It's impos-
sible to be exact, but I guess that it had been driven at least 50,000-
75,000 miles and I can say for sure that it was driven a lot of miles
on dirt.



                         Respectfully submitted,



                         Al "Honker" Green
                         February 3, 19___
```

Barbara quickly outlined the whole story for the judge and emphasized that she had saved for six months to get the money to make the purchase.*

Next, John had his turn. He helped Barbara make her case by acting like a weasel. His testimony consisted mostly of a lot of vague philosophy about machinery. He kept asking "how could I know just when it would break?" When the judge asked him specific questions about the age, condition and previous history of the cycle, he clammed up as if he was a mafioso called to testify by a Senate anti-racketeering committee. Finally, the judge in frustration asked John if he had anything concrete to say. John

---

* This sort of testimony isn't relevant, but it never hurts. As an old appeals court judge who had seen at least 75 summers told me when I graduated from law school and was proud of my technical mastery of the law, "Son, don't worry about the law — just convince the judge that truth and virtue are on your side and he will always find some technicality to support you." No one ever gave me better advice.

said yes and started explaining how when you sell things, you "puff them up a little" and that "women shouldn't be allowed to drive motorcycles anyway." Finally, the judge asked him to please sit down.

IMPORTANT: In this type of case, it's often one person's word against another's. Any shred of tangible evidence for either side can be enough to shift the balance to that side. Of course, if you have a friend who witnessed or heard any part of the transaction, his or her testimony will be extremely valuable. Getting a mechanic to check over a vehicle and then testify for you is also a good strategy. Sometimes you can get some help from the small blue book that lists wholesale and retail prices for used cars. Several times I have seen people bring this book (libraries and car dealers have them) into court and show the judge that they paid above the bluebook price for a used car "because the car was represented to be in extra good shape". This doesn't constitute much in the way of real proof that you were ripped off, but it is helpful to at least show the judge that you paid a premium price for unsound goods.

18

CASES WHERE MONEY IS OWED

A. FROM THE CREDITOR'S POINT OF VIEW

The job of the plaintiff in a case where he or she is suing for non-payment of a debt is to prove that a valid debt exists and that it has not been paid. Here are a few suggestions:

1. Sue Promptly
When you are owed money, be sure you sue promptly. You will find a discussion of the Statutes of Limitations applicable to different sorts of debts in Chapter 5. But even when there is no danger that the limitation period will run out, it makes sense to proceed as soon as reasonably possible. Judges just aren't as sympathetic to old claims. Several times when I have sat as judge, I have wondered why someone waited three years to sue for $500. Was it because he/she wasn't honestly convinced that his/her suit was valid?

2. Written Contracts
If the debt is based on a written contract, be sure that your paperwork is in order. Bring to court the original copy of any

written note proving the indebtedness so that the court can cancel it when the judgment is entered. Also bring any ledger sheets or other documentation as to any payments made, interest charged, etc. Often I have seen otherwise sensible looking business people show up with botched records and become flustered when closely questioned by the judge. The courtroom is not the place to straighten out a poor accounting system.

3. Oral Contracts

A debt based on an oral contract is legal as long as the contract could have been carried out in one year. However, you may face a problem proving that the debt exists if the defendant denies that he borrowed the money, or bought the goods. Your best bet is to come up with some written documentation that your version of the story is true. If you have no written evidence (cancelled checks, letters or notes asking for more time to pay , etc.), your next step is to try to think of any person who knows about the debt and who would be willing to testify. For example, if you asked the defendant to pay you and he said in the presence of your friend, "I'll pay you next month", or "You will never get your money back" or anything to indicate that a loan existed, bring your friend as a witness.

4. Proving Your Case

All too often a business will send the same bookkeeper-type to court for every case. He or she will be competent enough in establishing that the books say that the money is owed, but will be helpless if the defendant starts raising questions about anything else. For example, if you own a T.V. repair business and are suing on an unpaid repair bill in a situation where the defendant claims that you did lousy work, you will want someone in court who knows the details of the job. If you are incorporated, you can authorize the person who actually did the work to appear without the necessity of going yourself. As noted in Chapter 7, both incorporated and unincorporated businesses can send employees to represent them in court on claims involving unpaid bills, but in a case involving whether TV repairs were made, the owner of an unincorporated business would have to show up himself. Of course, he or she could bring the person who actually did the work as a witness. If you find yourself in court suing on a debt when you suddenly realize that you don't have the right witness in court, ask that the case be delayed a few days. Many judges will do this if they feel that you made a sincere effort to be ready, but something came up that you couldn't foresee.

NOTE: Many businesses, and especially professionals such as doctors, dentists and lawyers, don't use Small Claims Court to collect unpaid bills because they think it takes too much of their own time, or is "undignified". You will have to worry about your "dignity" yourself, but I can tell you that Small Claims Court actions can be handled with very little time and expense once you get the hang of it. This is especially true when you consider that the alternative is to turn the bill over to a collection agency or not to collect it at all. As long as the suit simply involves getting a judgment for an unpaid bill, you can send your bookkeeper to court. Wait until you have several cases and schedule them on the same day. Your employee should talk to the clerk when cases are set for hearing and make sure they are scheduled for a light court day. When your employee gets to court, he or she should speak to the clerk and point out that all your cases are defaults and see if it's possible to have them scheduled first. There is no need to be aggressive, but it never hurts to ask. You will find that, once your bookkeeper understands the system, he or she can often be in and out in fifteen minutes to a half hour. Once you get your judgment, your secretarial staff should be able to handle the collection activities described in Chapter 24.

B. FROM THE DEBTOR'S POINT OF VIEW

While there is an increasing number of private individuals using Small Claims Court, most plaintiffs trying to collect money are businesses or government entities, such as a library, hospital or city tax office. Debt case defendants are often individuals with little in their pockets but holes. Not many years ago, debt collection cases so numerically dominated Small Claims Court dockets that the court was in danger of becoming a "bill collectors' court". For a variety of reasons, perhaps the most important being the hopelessness of getting disputes resolved in more formal courts, Small Claims Courts have recently been used by a much wider variety of people to settle a broader range of disputes. This has been a healthy development and now the representatives of the department stores, tire companies and credit

144

jewelers are only part of the crowd.

When I first watched debt collection cases, I did so with scant attention. I assumed that individuals being pursued by large institutions were bound to lose, especially since they mostly did owe the money. I even wondered why a lot of folks bothered to show up — knowing in advance that they had no defense, and no money. I thought it unjust that our society divided its bounty so unfairly and sad that the poor had no better defense than their inability to pay. But then a curious thing happened. Many of the "downtrodden" I had dismissed so easily, refused to play their docile parts. Instead of shuffling in with heads down and nothing constructive to say, they argued back, stamped their feet and acted like the proud and dignified people they were. I realized suddenly that I was the only person in the courtroom that had dismissed them. I learned that morning, and on dozens of later mornings, that there are lots of ways to constructively defend non-payment of debt cases. Here are some examples:

A local hospital sued an unemployed man for failure to pay an emergency room bill for $278. It seemed an open and shut case — the person from the hospital had all the proper records, and the defendant hadn't paid. Then the defendant told his side of it. He was taken to the emergency room suffering from a gunshot wound. Because it was a busy night and he was not about to die, he was kept waiting four hours for treatment. When treatment was given, it was minimal and he suffered later complications that might have been avoided, if he had been treated promptly. He said he didn't mind paying a fair amount, but that he didn't feel he got $278 worth of care for seeing a doctor for half an hour. The judge agreed and gave judgment to the hospital for $90, plus court and service of process costs of $5.00. After the defendant explained that he had only his unemployment check, the judge ordered that he be allowed to pay off the judgment at the rate of $10 per month.

A large tire company sued a woman for not paying the balance on a tire bill. She had purchased eight tires for two pickup trucks and still owed $312.50. The tire company properly presented the judge with the original copy of a written contract along with the woman's payment record, and then waited for judgment. They are still waiting. The woman, who ran a small neighborhood gardening and landscaping business, produced several advertising flyers from the tire company which strongly implied, but didn't quite state, that the tires would last at least 40,000 miles. She then testified and presented a witness to the fact that the tires had only gone 25,000 miles before wearing out. The defendant also had copies of four letters written over the past year to the headquarters of the tire company in the Midwest complaining about the tires. Both in the letters, and in court, she repeatedly stated that the salesperson at the tire company told her several times that the tires were guaranteed for 40,000 miles. Putting this all together, the judge decided the tires should be prorated on the basis of 40,000 miles and gave the tire company a judgment for only $102, instead of the $312.50 requested. The woman wrote them out a check on the spot and departed feeling vindicated.

A rug company sued a customer for $686 and produced all the necessary documentation showing that the carpet had been installed, but no payment received. The defendant testified that the rug had been poorly installed with an uneven seam running down the center of the room. He had pictures that left no doubt that the rug layer was either drunk or blind. The defendant also presented drawings that illustrated that there were obviously several better ways to cut the carpet to fit the room. The rug company received nothing.

146

The point of these examples is not the facts of the individual situations — yours will surely differ. The point is that there are all sorts of defenses, and partial defenses, and that it makes sense to defend yourself creatively if you feel that goods or services you received were worth less than you are being sued for. It is usually not enough to tell the judge that you were dissatisfied with what you received. A little more imagination is required. If shoddy goods are involved, show them to the judge. If you received bad service, bring a witness or other supporting evidence. If, for example, you got roof repairs done that resulted in more holes than you had before, take pictures of the rain leaking in, and get an estimate from another roofer.

There is often a tactical advantage for the debtor in the fact that the person who appears in court on behalf of the creditor is not the same person that he had dealings with. If, for example, you state that a salesperson told you X, Y and Z, that person probably won't be present to state otherwise. This may tilt a closely balanced case to you. It is not inappropriate for you to point out to the judge that your opponent has only books and ledgers and no first hand knowledge of the situation. The judge may sometimes continue the case until another day to allow the creditor to have whatever employee(s) you dealt with present, but often this is impossible because the employee in question will have left the job, or be otherwise unavailable.

A LITTLE MORE TIME TO PAY: In California (Code of Civil Procedure 117) and in many other states, the judge has considerable discretion to order that a judgment be paid in installments. Thus, a judge could find that you owe the phone company $200, but allow you to pay it off at $20 per month, instead of all at once. Time payments can be particularly helpful if you don't have the money to pay all at once, but fear a wage attachment or other collection activity by the creditor. Don't be afraid to ask the judge for time payments — he or she won't know that you want them if you don't. People who owe money and want to learn more about their legal rights in such areas as attachments, bankruptcy, dealing with collection agencies, etc., should see *The California Debtors' Handbook – Billpayers' Rights,* Honigsberg and Warner, Nolo Press.

19

VEHICLE ACCIDENT CASES

It is a rare Small Claims session that does not include at least one fender bender. Usually these cases are badly prepared and presented. The judge commonly makes a decision at least partially by guess. I know from personal experience that it sometimes wouldn't take much additional evidence for me to completely reverse a decision. In Chapter 2, I discuss the concept of negligence and what's involved in proving it. Re-read this chapter before proceeding.

The average vehicle accident that ends up in Small Claims Court doesn't involve personal injury, but is concerned with damage to one, or both, parties' car, cycle, r.v., moped or whatever.* Because of some quirk of character that seems to be deeply embedded in our overgrown monkey brains, it is almost impossible for most of us to admit that we are bad drivers, or are at fault in a car accident. We will cheerfully acknowledge that we aren't terrific looking or geniuses, but we all believe that we drive like angels. Out of fantasies such as these lawsuits are made.

---

* Cases involving all but the most minor personal injuries don't belong in Small Claims Court as they will result in settlements of more than the Small Claims maximum.

A. WHO CAN SUE WHOM?

The owner of a vehicle must sue for damage to the vehicle, even if he wasn't driving when the damage occurred. Any person injured whether driver, passenger or pedestrian must sue for his or her own personal injuries. Suit should be brought against the negligent driver and, if the driver is not the registered owner of the car, the registered owner too. Both the driver and the registered owner are liable. To find out who owns a car, contact the Department of Motor Vehicles. As long as you can tell them the license number, they can tell you the registered owner.

Be particularly wary when you are opposing a bus or truck driver. Many of these people suffer problems on their jobs if they are found to be at fault in too many accidents. As a result they deny fault almost automatically. Judges usually know this and are often unsympathetic when a bus driver says that there has never been a time when he "didn't look both ways twice, count to ten and say the Lord's Prayer" before pulling out from a bus stop. Still, it never hurts to question the driver in court as to whether his company has any demerit system or other penalty for being at fault in an accident.

B. WAS THERE A WITNESS TO THE ACCIDENT?

Because the judge has no way of knowing what happened unless one or more people tell him (her), a good witness can make or break your case. It is better to have a disinterested witness than a close friend or family member, but any witness is better than no witness. If the other guy is likely to have a witness and you have none, you will have to work extra hard to develop other evidence to overcome this advantage. Re-read Chapter 14 for more information on witnesses.

C. POLICE ACCIDENT REPORTS

It is always wise to have a police accident report prepared after any accident. They are admissible as evidence in Small Claims Court. The theory is that a cop investigating the circumstances of the accident at the scene is in a better position to establish the truth of what happened than is any other third party. So, if there is an accident report, buy a copy for a few dollars from the police station. If it supports you, bring it to court. If it doesn't, be prepared to refute what it says. This can best be done with the testimony of an eye witness. If both an eye witness and a police report are against you, try prayer.

D. DIAGRAMS

After witnesses and police accident reports, the most effective evidence is a good diagram. It is almost impossible for a judge to understand how an accident happened using words alone. Several times I have seen a good case lost because the judge never properly visualized what happened. All courtrooms have blackboards, and it is proper to draw out what happened as part of your presentation. If you are nervous about your ability to do this, you may want to prepare your diagram in advance and bring it to court. Use crayons or magic markers and draw on a large piece of paper about three feet square . Do a good job with attention to detail. Here is a sample drawing that you might prepare to aid your testimony if you were eastbound on Rose St. and making a right hand turn on Sacramento St. when you were hit by a car that ran a stop sign on Sacramento. Of course, the diagram doesn't tell the whole story — you have to do that.

E. PHOTOS

Photographs can sometimes be of aid in fender bender cases. They can serve to back up your story about how an accident occurred. For example, if you claimed that you were sideswiped while you were parked, a photo showing a long series of scratches down the side of your car would be helpful. It is also a good idea to have a pictures of the defendant's car if you can manage to get them and photos of the scene of the accident.

F. ESTIMATES

In a vehicle accident case you are entitled to recover for damage to your vehicle, personal injuries, uncompensated time off from work as a result of personal injuries, damages to things inside your car, and money for transportation while your car was out-of-commission.* Of course, major accidents will not be heard in Small Claims Court, and most Small Claims cases involve only damage to a vehicle. Get three written estimates for the cost of repairing the vehicle. If you have already gotten the work done, bring your cancelled check or receipt from the repair shop. Be sure to get your estimates from reputable shops. If, for some reason, you get an estimate from someone you later think isn't competent, simply ignore it, and get another. You have no responsibility to get your car fixed by anyone suggested to you by the person who caused the damage. Common sense normally dictates that you don't. Unfortunately, you can't recover money from the other party to cover the time you put in to get estimates, take your car to the repair shop, or appear in court.

DEFENDANT'S NOTE: Sometimes plaintiffs dishonestly try to get already existing damage to their car fixed as part of getting the legitimate accident work done. If you think the repair bill is high, try developing your own evidence that this is so. If you have a picture of the plaintiff's car showing the damage, this can be a big help. Also, remember that the plaintiff is only entitled to get repairs made up to the total value of the car before the accident. If the car was worth only $500 and the repairs would cost $750, the plaintiff is only entitled to $500 (see Chapter 5).

G. YOUR DEMAND LETTER

Here again, as in almost every other type of Small Claims Court case, you should write a letter to your opponent with an eye to the judge reading it. See the examples in Chapter 6. Here is another:

---

* See Chapter 5 for a more thorough discussion of damages. As far as getting money for transportation while your car is out-of-commission, you can only recover for the minimum time it would take to get your car fixed. Thus, if you could arrange to get a fender put right in one day, you are only entitled to a rent-a-car for one day, even if the mechanic takes four.

In court Sandy would present her case like this:

Clerk: "Next case, McClatchy v. Rugg. Please come forward."

Judge: "Please tell me what happened, Ms. McClatchy."

Sandy McClatchy: "Good morning. This dispute involves an auto acci-dent that occureed at Rose and Sacramento Streets on the afternoon of August 15, 19—. I was coming uphill on Rose (that's east) and stopped at the corner. There is a four-way stop sign at the corner. I turned right, or south, on Sacramento Street, and as I was doing so, Mr. Rugg ran the stop sign on Sacramento and crashed into my front fender. Your Honor, may I use the blackboard to make a quick diagram?"

Judge: "Please do, I was about to ask you if you would."

Sandy McClatchy: (Makes drawing like the one in D above, points out the movement of the cars in detail and answers several questions from the judge.) "Your Honor, before I sit down, I would like to give you several items of evidence. First, I have a copy of the police accident report from the Fullerton police which states that Mr. Rugg got a citation for failing to stop at a stop sign. Second, I have some photos which show the damage to the front fender of my car. Third, I have my letter to Mr. Rugg, trying to settle this case and finally I have several estimates for the cost of repairing the damage to my car. As you can see from my cancelled check, I took the lowest one."

Judge: "Thank you, Ms. McClatchy. Now, Mr. Rugg, it's your turn."

R. Rigsby Rugg: "Your Honor, my case rests on one basic fact. Ms. McClatchy was negligent because she made a wide turn into Sacramento Street. Instead of going from the right hand lane of Rose to the right hand, or inside lane, on Sacramento Street, she turned into the center lane on Sacramento Street. (Mr. Rugg moves to the blackboard and points out what he says happened.) Now it might be true that I made a rolling stop at the corner. You know, I really stopped, but maybe not quite all the way — but I never would have hit anybody if she had kept to her own side of the road. Also, your Honor, I would like to say this — she darted out; she has one of those little foreign cars and instead of easing out slow like I do with my Lincoln, she jumped out like a rabbit being chased by a red fox."

Judge: "Do you have anything else to say, Ms. McClatchy?"

Sandy McClatchy: "I am not going to even try to argue about whether Mr. Rugg can be rolling and stopped at the same time. I think the policeman who cited him answered that question. I want to answer his point about my turning into the center lane on Sacramento St., instead of the inside lane. It is true that, after stopping, I had to make a slightly wider turn than usual. If you will look again at the diagram I drew, you will see that a car was parked almost to the corner of Sacramento and Rose on Sacramento. To get around this car, I had to drive a little farther into Sacramento before starting my turn than would have been necessary otherwise. I didn't turn into the center lane, but as I made the turn, my outside fender crossed into the center lane slightly. This is when Mr. Rugg hit me. I feel that since I had the right of way and I had to do what I did to make the turn, I wasn't negligent."

Judge: "Thank you both — you will get my decision in the mail."

(The judge decided in favor of Sandy McClatchy and awarded her $412 plus service of process and filing costs.)

NOTE: As I discussed in Chapter 5, you can win, or partially win, a case involving negligence even if you were not completely in the right. If the other person was more at fault than you were, you have a case. This concept of "comparative" negligence is a new one in California. It used to be that, if you were even a little at fault, you couldn't recover.

20

LANDLORD-TENANT CASES

Small Claims Court can be used by a tenant to sue for money damages for such things as the failure of a landlord to return a cleaning or damage deposit. A landlord might use it to sue a tenant or former tenant for damage done to the rental property. In some situations it is also possible for a landlord to seek to evict a tenant. This is an exception to the general rule that only money judgments can be handed down by Small Claims Courts. It makes great sense to use Small Claims Court for money damage cases, and a lot less sense to use it for evictions. Evictions are usually handled better in Municipal Court. Why? Because, in Small Claims Court, the defendant has an automatic right to appeal the eviction judgment and to remain living in the rental unit while the appeal is pending even though no rent is paid (see Section C below). This rule badly needs changing. Indeed, a lot of rules need changing so that all landlord-tenant cases can automatically be heard in a special division of Small Claims Court. Landlord and tenant both should have quick access to an inexpensive dispute resolution forum where hassles can be settled quickly, cheaply and fairly.

A. DEPOSIT CASES

The most common landlord-tenant disputes concern the failure of a landlord to return a tenant's cleaning and damage deposits after the tenant moves out. These days, deposits can add up to many hundreds of dollars and tenants understandably want them returned.

Getting deposits back can be easy or difficult depending upon both the facts of the situation and on how much homework a tenant has done in advance of filing suit. Many landlords are experienced with Small Claims proceedings and come to court prepared with a long list of damaged and dirty conditions that they claim that the tenant left behind. All too often, the landlord's presentation leaves the tenant sputtering with righteous indignation. Unfortunately evidence, not indignation, wins cases. Think about it — if the tenant testifies that the apartment was clean, and the landlord that it was dirty, the judge (unless he or she is psychic) is stuck making a decision that is little more than a guess. Faced with this sort of situation, most judges will split the difference.

How should a tenant prepare a case involving failure to return deposits? Ideally, preparation should start when he or she moves in. Any damage or dirty conditions should be noted as part of the lease or rental agreement. The tenant should also take photographs of substandard conditions and have neighbors or friends look the place over. When the tenant moves out and cleans up, he (she) should do much the same thing — take photos, have friends check the place over, keep receipts for cleaning materials and try to reach an understanding with the landlord.*

In California the burden of proof that conditions exist which justify the landlord keeping all, or part, of a deposit falls on the landlord. The law also states that, if a deposit is not returned within two weeks from the time the tenant moves out and if the landlord acted in bad faith in retaining the deposits, the tenant may be entitled to $200 in "punitive" damages, over and above the actual amount of the deposits.** Whether or not the tenant actually gets punitive damages is a matter of judicial discretion,

---

* All of this is discussed in more detail in *The California Tenants' Handbook*, Moskovitz, Warner and Sherman (order information at back of this book). The *Tenants' Handbook* contains a tear-out room-by-room inventory sheet so that landlord and tenant can inspect the place on moving in and moving out and jointly record the results.
** California Civil Code 1950.5.

but it never hurts to bring your suit for an amount that includes them.

Now let's assume that you are a tenant and have not gotten $300 in cleaning and damage deposits returned even though you moved out of an apartment three weeks ago, having paid all your rent and having given proper notice. Start by writing the landlord a letter like this:

```
                                        1700 Walnut Street
                                        Costa Mesa, Calif.

                                        October 15, 19___


Anderson Realty Co.
10 Rose St.
Costa Mesa, Calif.

Dear People:

     As you know, until September 30, 19___, I resided in apartment #4 at
1700 Walnut Street and regularly paid my rent to your office.  When I
moved out, I left the unit cleaner than when I moved in.

     As of today, I have received neither my $150 cleaning deposit nor my
$150 damage deposit.  Indeed I have never received any accounting from
you for any of my money.  Please be aware that I know my rights under
California Civil Code 1950.5 and that, if I do not receive my money
within the next week, I will regard the retention of these deposits as
showing "bad faith" on your part and shall sue you, not only for the
$300 in deposits, but also for the $200 punitive damages allowed by Sec-
tion 1950.5 of the California Civil Code.

     May I hear from you soon.



                                        Sincerely,


                                        Farah Shields
```

If you get no satisfactory response, file your case. Sometimes it is hard to know who to sue as rent isn't always paid to the owner, but to a manager or other agent. In California multiple occupancy buildings must have ownership information posted on the premises, or have the name of the owner or his agent for suit, on the rental agreement. If you are in doubt as to who owns your unit, you are probably safe if you sue both the person to whom you pay your rent, and the person who signed the rental agreement, unless you have received notice that the building has been transferred to a new owner, in which case you would sue that person.

On court day a well-prepared tenant would show up in court with as many of the following pieces of evidence as possible:

• Photos of the apartment on moving in which show any dirt or damage that already existed.

• Photos of the apartment on moving out which show clean conditions.

• Receipts for cleaning supplies used in the final clean-up.

• A copy of your written lease or rental agreement, if any.

• A copy of a demand letter to the landlord such as the one set out above.

• One, or preferably two, witnesses who were familiar with the property and saw it after you cleaned up and who will testify that it was immaculate. People who helped in the clean-up are always particularly effective witnesses. If you also have a witness who saw the place when you moved in and who will say that it wasn't so clean (or damage already existed), so much the better.

• A copy of an inventory of conditions when moving in and moving out, signed by the landlord and tenant, if one was prepared.

Proceedings in court should go something like this:

Clerk: "Shields v. Anderson Realty. Please step forward."

Judge: "Good morning. Please tell me your version of the facts, Ms. Shields."

Farah Shields: "I moved into the cottage at 1700 Walnut St. in Costa Mesa in the spring of 1978. I paid Mr. Anderson here my first and last months' rent which totaled $400. I also paid him $300 in deposits. The deposits were divided $150 for cleaning and $150 for damage. Here is a copy of the rental agreement (hands it to the clerk) which specifically states that these deposits are to be returned to me if the apartment is left clean and undamaged.

When I moved into 1700 Walnut, it was a mess. It's a nice little cottage, but the people who lived there before me were sloppy. The stove was filthy, as was the bathroom, the refrigerator, the floors and just about everything else. In addition, the walls hadn't been painted in years. But I needed a place and this was the best available, so I moved in despite the mess. I painted the whole place — everything. Mr. Anderson's office gave me the paint, but I did all of the work. And I cleaned the place thoroughly too. It took me three days. I like to live in a clean house.

Here are some pictures of what the place looked like when I moved in (hands photos to clerk who gives them to the judge). Here is a second set of photos which were taken after I moved out and cleaned up (again hands pictures to clerk). Your Honor, I think these pictures tell the story — the place was clean when I moved out. I also have receipts (hands to clerk) for cleaning supplies and a rug shampooer that I used during the clean-up. They total $18.25. I have also brought two people who saw the place the day I left and can tell you what it looked like."

Judge: (looking at one of the witnesses) "Do you have some personal knowledge of what this cottage looked like?"

John DeBono: "Yes, I helped Farah move in and move out. I simply don't understand what the landlord is fussing about. The place was a smelly mess when she moved in, and it was spotless when Farah moved out."

Judge: (addressing the second witness) "Do you have something to add?"

Puna Polaski: "I never saw 1700 Walnut when Farah moved in because I didn't know her then. But I did help her pack and clean up when she moved out. I can tell you that the windows were washed, the floor waxed and the oven cleaned because I did it. And I can tell you that the rest of the cottage was clean too, because I saw it."

Judge: "Mr. Anderson, do you want to present your case?"

Adam Anderson: "Your Honor, I am not here to argue about whether the place was clean or not. Maybe it was cleaner when Miss Shields moved out than when she moved in. The reason I withheld the deposits is that the walls were all painted odd, bright colors and I have had to paint them all over. Here are some color pictures of the walls taken just after Miss Shields moved out. They show several pink, light blue and purple rainbows, a dancing hedgehog, six birds apparently laughing, a purple dog, and several unicorns of various sizes. I ask you, your Honor, how was I going to rent that place with a purple bulldog painted on the living room wall, especially with an orange butterfly on his nose. It cost me more than $300 to have the place painted over white."

Judge: (looks at the pictures and gives up trying to keep a straight face which is OK as everyone in the courtroom is laughing except Mr. Anderson) "Let me ask a few questions. Was it true that the place needed a new coat of paint when you moved in, Ms. Shields?"

Farah Shields: "Yes."

Judge: "Do you agree, Mr. Anderson?"

Adam Anderson: "Yes, that's why my office paid her paint bills although we never would have if we had known about that bulldog, not to mention the rainbows."

Judge: "How much did the paint cost?"

Adam Anderson: "$65."

Judge: "I normally send decisions by mail, but today I am going to explain what I have decided. First, the apartment needed repainting anyway, Mr. Anderson, so I am not going to give you any credit for paying to have the work done. However, Ms. Shields, even though the place looks quite — shall I say, cheerful — decorated with its assorted wildlife, Mr. Anderson does have a point in that you went a little beyond what is reasonable. Therefore, I feel that it's unfair to make Anderson Realty pay for paint twice. My judgment is this: The $65 for the paint that was given to Ms. Shields is subtracted from the $300 deposits. This means that Anderson Realty owes Farah Shields $235 plus $4.00 for costs.

NOTE: We have focused here on deposit cases from the tenant's point of view. This is because tenants are the ones who initiate this sort of case. Landlords, too though, should gain by carefully reading the list of evidence that is helpful in court. Often the best witness for a landlord is the new tenant who has just moved in. This person is likely to feel that the place isn't as clean as did the person who moved out.

B. MONEY DAMAGE CASES — UNPAID RENT

Landlords most commonly initiate Small Claims actions to sue for unpaid rent. Often the tenant has already moved out and doesn't bother to show up in court. If this happens, the landlord wins by default. Sometimes the tenant does show up, but presents no real defense and is only there to request the judge to allow him to make payments over time (see Chapter 23 B).

The landlord should bring the lease or rental agreement to court and simply state the time periods for which rent is due, but unpaid. Nothing else is required unless the tenant claims that he did pay the rent. Sometimes a landlord will sue for three times the amount of rent owed (triple damages) under a lease or rental agreement that states that he is entitled to them if the tenant fails to pay rent, but stays in the rental unit. Doing this will almost guarantee that the tenant will put up a fight. In my experience landlords are rarely awarded more than their actual out-of-pocket loss, and it makes little sense to request more.

There are several valid defenses to a suit based on a tenant's failure to pay rent. The principal one is where the tenant claims that rent was withheld because the condition of the premises was "uninhabitable".* This amounts to the tenant saying to the landlord: "I won't pay my rent until you make necessary repairs".** It is legal to do this in California under the decision in Green v. Superior Court, 10 CAL 3d 616.*** The important thing for a tenant to understand is that rent withholding is not legal where the landlord refuses to fix some minor defect. For rent to be legally withheld, the condition needing repair must be sufficiently serious as to make the home "uninhabitable". In addition, the landlord must have been given reasonable notice of the problem. Thus, a broken furnace that a landlord refused to fix would qualify as a condition making a home uninhabitable in the winter, but lack of heat in the summer would not.

If you are involved in a rent withholding case as a tenant, your job is to prove (pictures, witnesses, etc.) that the condition that caused you to withhold rent is indeed serious. Thus, you might call the building inspector or an electrician to testify that the wiring was in a dangerous state of decay. The landlord, of course, has to prove the opposite — that the rental unit is in fundamentally sound shape, even though there may be some minor problems. A landlord has the right to inspect his (her) properties at reasonable hours of the day as long as he (she) gives the tenant

---

* Under California law it is also legal for a tenant to have repairs done himself under some circumstances and deduct the cost from one month's rent. See California Civil Code Section 1941-42. This "repair and deduct" remedy is also discussed in detail in The California Tenants' Handbook.
** Often a tenant who fails to pay rent is brought to court by the landlord as part of an eviction action. If the tenant can prove that rent was withheld for a valid reason, he or she can't be evicted for exercising this right in California.
*** If you are outside of California, check with a tenants' rights project or consumer group before withholding rent. Not all states allow rent withholding even when conditions are awful. If you are in California, see The California Tenants' Handbook, Moskovitz, Warner and Sherman, which goes into rent withholding and retaliation eviction in detail.

reasonable notice. In California, 24 hours' notice is presumed by the law to be reasonable in the absence of an emergency. The landlord cannot use his (her) right to inspect to harass the tenant, but the law has set down no absolute guidelines as to what harassment is.

NOTE: In place of the present cumbersome procedure which does not allow a tenant to sue to get needed repairs made in Small Claims Court, but instead requires him first to withhold rent and then defend himself in an eviction action, we need to reform our landlord-tenant law to provide for an effective procedure which tenants can institute when a landlord abdicates his responsibility to properly maintain rental property.

C. EVICTIONS

Without question landlords should have a simple and cheap way to free themselves of tenants who don't pay their rent. If a landlord wants to be sure to get a tenant out without ridiculous delays, an "unlawful detainer" action must be filed in Municipal Court. Traditionally, this has required the expense of a lawyer. There is now a book, *A Legal Guide for California Landlords*, D. Brown, available through Nolo Press* in December 1981, which tells landlords how to fill out the Municipal Court papers themselves.

As I said above, it is legal to do some types of evictions in Small Claims Court. This includes the situation where a tenant of residential property has a written or oral, month-to-month (or week-to-week) rental agreement and is behind in the rent.** If a lease is involved giving the tenant a set term of occupancy longer than 30 days, or if the eviction is for some reason other than non-payment of rent, the eviction action cannot be brought in Small Claims Court.

The form necessary to bring an "unlawful detainer" (eviction) action in Small Claims Court looks like this. (The form for Municipal Court is quite different.)

---

* See back of this book for order information.

** Before the landlord files an unlawful detainer (eviction) action, he or she must first serve the defendant (tenant) with a three-day notice to pay rent or leave the premises. A carbon of this notice should be retained to show the Small Claims Court. Only after the three-day notice has run out can an "unlawful detainer" be filed. The three-day notice may be personally served on the tenant by the landlord himself or by anyone else. In the alternative, a copy may be left at the defendant's address with a responsible person and another copy mailed to him. A proof of service should be filled out (see Chapter 11).

SMALL CLAIMS COURT OF CALIFORNIA, COUNTY OF ALAMEDA

BERKELEY - ALBANY JUDICIAL DISTRICT
2000 Center St. Berkeley, 94704

SC. NO (Fill in #)

PLAINTIFF   DEFENDANT

● John Landlord   ● Tillie Tenant
  33 Orange   160 11th St.
  Berkeley, CA.   Berkeley, CA.

CLAIM OF PLAINTIFF

FOR UNLAWFUL DETAINER

John Landlord
(Name of Declarant or Plaintiff)

declare that prior to SERVICE OF 3 DAY NOTICE,
defendant(s) were tenants of plaintiff(s) in the premises described as _160 11th St., Berkeley, CA._

_____, California, at a rental of $ _200.00_
per _month_ , payable _on the 1st_ ; that on _December 25_ defendant(s) were
indebted to plaintiff(s) in the sum of $ _$175.00_ ; as rent for said premises; that on _Dec. 21_
plaintiff(s) served the attached notice on defendant(s); that defendant(s) have not paid any part of the rent demanded and are still in possession of the premises without consent of plaintiff(s); that the rental value of said
premises is $ _200.00_ per month. **THIS CLAIMANT UNDERSTANDS THAT THE JUDGMENT ON
HIS CLAIM WILL BE CONCLUSIVE WITHOUT RIGHT OF APPEAL.**
I declare under penalty of perjury that the foregoing is true and correct.

Executed on _Dec. 25_ at _Berkeley_
(Date)   (Place)   (Plaintiff or Declarant)
(Signature of landlord)

ORDER

The people of the State of California, to the within named defendant:
You are hereby directed to appear and answer the within and foregoing claim at the above entitled Court in Department_____,
at _____ M. On _____ ,and to have with you, then and there all books, papers and witnesses needed by
you to establish your defense to said claim. And you are further notified that in case you do not so appear, judgment will be given
against you in accordance with said claim as it is stated in said declaration and in addition costs of the action including costs of
service of the order.

, CLERK

DATED_____   BY_____
                                                                                    DEPUTY CLERK

Date_____	Hearing reset for _____	,at _____ M .Dept _____
Date_____	Hearing reset for _____	,at _____ M .Dept _____
Date_____	Hearing reset for _____	,at _____ M .Dept _____

Date of Proceeding	Proceedings (applicable only when dated and/or checked in box)	FEES, COSTS, ETC	
		AMOUNT	RECEIPT NO
	Claim of Plaintiff, fees paid, order issued		
	Order and copy of declaration Mailed to defendant(s) by certified mail ☐		
	Delivered to Plaintiff for personal service ☐		

DOCKET COPY

FORM NO 170-199   ⊚ 463000

Why, if some evictions can be brought in Small Claims Court,
isn't it wise to do so? Because what seems simple can often become cumbersome and complicated. Remember, the defendant-
tenant has an automatic right to appeal from a Small Claims
judgment. If he exercises this right in an eviction action, he can

stay living in the property while the case is transferred to the Superior Court. A tenant who knows the rules can often delay eviction three or four months by simply appealing the Small Claims eviction decision, even though he pays no rent and has no chance of winning the case in Superior Court.

Of course, the worst doesn't always happen. Many times a tenant who is served with Small Claims eviction papers moves out without a fight. If this occurs, you are ahead of the game and have saved time over the Municipal Court procedure. It's a bit of a gamble, although you may be able to shorten the odds a little by giving some thought to the personality and sophistication of your tenant. If you think he or she is going to try to hold on to the apartment like a tick to a tasty dog, you had better go to Municipal Court.

When a landlord gets to court, he need only prove that the rent was not paid and that a correct three-day notice was properly served.* Bring a copy of the three-day notice to court and a "proof of service" form filled out by the person doing the service. The fact that a tenant is suffering from some hardship such as illness, poverty, birth of a child, etc., is not a defense to failure to pay rent. Possible tenant defenses are discussed briefly in Section B of this chapter. These include rent withholding and a tenant repairing an item himself (herself) and deducting the cost from the rent. A tenant cannot legally raise a defect for the first time on the day of the court hearing. The landlord must be given reasonable notice that a defect exists before rent is withheld, or repairs are made.

---

* Under California law when a tenant fails to pay rent, a landlord must first serve him (her) with a three-day notice to either pay the rent or leave the premises. The notice must be in the alternative — a notice that simply tells the tenant to get out is not legal and can be challenged later by the tenant in court. Only after a proper three-day notice has run out can the landlord legally start his eviction action.

21

SMALL BUSINESS, SMALL CLAIMS

More and more, people who own or manage small businesses are turning to Small Claims Court to settle business disputes that they have been unable to compromise. They have learned that Small Claims Court is a relatively fast and cost efficient way to resolve business differences. Recent law changes allowing unincorporated businesses to appear in court in some circumstances without the need for the owners to be present have contributed to this increase in business usage (see Chapter 7).*

This chapter didn't appear in the first few editions of this book because I naively assumed that Chapter 18 — CASES IN WHICH MONEY IS OWED — provided sufficient information to solve the problems of business people. It's here now because I have had so many requests from friends who own their own small business asking for additional information. It turned out, of course, that although many disputes between small business people involve a simple failure to pay money, a significant number are much more

---

* Of course, incorporated businesses have long been able to authorize people other than the officers or other principals to appear in court (see Chapter 4).

complicated. Commonly these more complex disputes involve people who have had a continuing business relationship and find themselves in the midst of a major misunderstanding that goes beyond the refusal to pay a bill. Often both parties to the law suit are in court because they feel badly used — perhaps even "ripped off" or "cheated" by the other.

I have been asked for advice on preparing Small Claims Court cases by a surprising variety of business people. Requests for help have come from a dentist furious at a dental equipment wholesaler, an industrial designer who hadn't been paid for drawing preliminary plans, a typesetter being sued by his former accountant in a dispute involving the value of the latter's services, a landscape architect who was trying to enforce a verbal contract to increase his fee after a client asked for changes in final plans, and an author who claimed that her publisher had taken too long to publish her book. Although these disputes seem quite different from one another at first impression, they all turned out to have one thing in common — in each situation the disputants had enjoyed friendly business relationships at some time in the past. And in each case, at least part of the reason that the plaintiff brought the dispute to court involved feelings of anger and hurt.

A. ORGANIZING YOUR CASE

Business people normally have two great advantages over ordinary mortals when it comes to preparing for court. First, as a matter of course, they maintain a record-keeping system which includes files, ledgers, and increasingly, floppy discs. Taken together, these resources normally contain considerable raw material helpful to successfully proving even a fairly complicated case. The second advantage is more subtle, but no less real. It involves the average small business person's organizational skill — that is, his or her ability to take a confused mess of facts and organize them into a coherent and convincing narrative. Small business people who don't quickly develop good organizational skills commonly aren't in business long enough to even consider going to court. But the fact that business people begin with a little head start isn't usually much of an advantage when it comes to dealing with another business person. This is because two head starts have a way of cancelling one another out, with the only beneficiary being the judge, who gets to officiate a shorter, more coherent dispute.

Here are several hints that may be of real value when thinking about how to present a business case. This material is meant to supplement, not replace, the information contained in the rest of the book, particularly Chapters 2, 6, 13, 14, and 15. If you haven't already done so, I think you will find it helpful to read these chapters before continuing.

1. Contracts

Most business cases involve one person claiming that the other has broken a contract (see Chapter 2). Ask yourself the exact nature of the contract which was involved in your case. That is, what were your obligations and benefits from the deal, what was the other person supposed to do, and what was he or she going to get out of the deal?

Remember that oral contracts that can be carried out in one year (even if they actually take longer) are legal and enforceable in California. But remember too that oral contracts raise real problems in proving the facts.

You should also remember that a written contract need not be a formal document written on parchment and notarized by the Dalai Lama. Any letter or writing can constitute a contract. For example, if Hubert writes to Josephine, "I would like to order 1000 gopher traps at $14.00 per trap," and Josephine writes back saying, "Thank you for your order. The traps will be sent next week," there is a contract. Indeed, if Josephine didn't write back at all but simply sent the traps in a reasonable period of time, there would also be a contract.

You should also be aware that the business usage and practices in a particular field are commonly viewed as being part of a contract and can be introduced as evidence in Small Claims Court to support your case. Thus, if Hubert ordered rodent traps in February and Josephine didn't send them until September, Hubert could present evidence in court that everyone in the rodent control business knows that traps are only saleable in the summer when rodents attack crops and that Josephine's failure to deliver the traps in the correct season constituted a breach of contract.

And keep in mind that contracts can be, and often are, changed many times as negotiations go back and forth and circumstances change. The important agreement is the last one.

2. Presenting Your Evidence in Court

a. Reread Chapter 15.

b. In business disputes, the problem is often having too much evidence, rather than too little. If this occurs, your job is obviously to separate the material that is essential to proving your case from that which is less important. One good way to do this is to organize both your verbal presentation and the back-up evidence around the central issue in dispute rather than trying to fill in all the background in an effort to work up to the point. Or, to say the same thing in a different way, you usually want to start with the end of your case rather than the beginning. For example, if Ted did interior decorating work for Alice and she called off the deal in the middle, Ted would start his testimony with the fact that a contract had existed to do the work and that Alice broke it. The fact that Ted and Alice had had dealings over the last several years which cast light on the present dispute, or that Ted had turned down another job to work for Alice, or that Alice had made a number of unreasonable demands on him, might well constitute good supporting evidence, but should be alluded to only to the extent that they support the main point. All too often I have seen people tell a great but lengthy story in court, only to put the judge to sleep before the main point was reached.

c. Many business people have employees, partners, or business associates who have intimate knowledge of the dispute. By all means, bring them to court as witnesses. A live witness is almost always worth more than a stack of documentary evidence.

d. In some situations, having a witness testify as to the normal business practices in a field can be helpful. Thus, if in your business payment is always made within thirty days after delivery of goods, and the person you are having a dispute with claimed that a 120-day payment schedule was adequate, you would want to present an "expert" witness who could testify as to normal business practices.

B. THE DRAMA OF THE DISTRAUGHT DESIGNER

Now let's review a case that I was recently asked about. Don is a successful industrial designer who heads his own small company. He has offices in a converted factory building near a major university and prides himself on doing highly innovative and creative work. Normally he is confident and cheerful, but one day when he stopped by the Nolo office to say hello, he looked more than a little out of sorts.

"What's up?" I asked.

"Oh, a couple of late nights of high pressure work," Don replied.

"What's new about that?" I asked him.

"Well, that's not really what's bugging me. Actually, I wonder if you can give me a little advice."

"Sure, what's the problem?"

"Well, I did some design work for an outfit that wants to build a small candle factory and I'm out $1,300. They claim that we never had a contract, but that's simply not true. What really happened is that they gambled and authorized me to do some preliminary work before they got their financing assured. When interest rates went through the roof, the whole deal collapsed. I had already completed my work, but they got uptight and refused to pay."

"So what are you going to do?" I asked him.

"Well, I got Stephanie Carlin, a lawyer who has done some work for me, to write them a letter, but that didn't do any good, so I took Stephanie's advice and filed a Small Claims Court suit against them myself."

"For how much?"

"For the Small Claims maximum. I had to scale down the claim to fit it in, but it was better than paying Stephanie $75 an hour."

"How can I help?" I asked.

"Believe it or not, I've never been to court and I'm afraid I will overlook something or do something stupid, like calling the judge 'your holiness' instead of 'your honor.' I'm not much on bowing and scraping and the whole court rigmarole has always annoyed me."

"Okay, let me show you how simple your job is. First, how did the candle people (let's call them Wickless) contact you to set up the deal?"

"They are friends of friends. They called and we talked on the phone a couple of times. There was a lot of back and forth about how much I would charge for the whole job and how much for parts of it. After a little ordinary confusion, we decided that I would start with the preliminary drawings and be paid thirteen hundred dollars. If the whole job came through and we felt good about one another, I would do the whole thing."

"Did you write up a contract?"

"No, that's just it. On big jobs I always do, but this one was tiny. They just stopped by the next day and we hashed out the whole thing in person."

"Did you make notes?"

"Sure. In fact, I made a few sketches and then they gave me specifications and sketches they had made."

"Do you still have those?"

"Yes, and also a couple of letters they sent later thanking me for my good ideas and making a few suggestions for changes. And of course, I have copies of the detailed drawings I made and sent them."

"Well, that's it then," I said.

"What do you mean, that's it? You mean that I don't have a case?"

170

"Just the contrary. I mean you have just told me that you can prove that a contract exists. The combination of the sketches they provided and the letters they wrote you pretty well prove that they asked you to do the work. There is a strong presumption in law that when a person is asked to do work, he or she is to be paid if the work is completed. Now, in this sort of situation, I suspect that Wickless will raise one of two defenses if they bother to contest your claim at all. The first is that you were doing your work on speculation — that is, that the deal was that you were to be paid for your preliminary work only if the financing went through, and/or second, that your work was substandard in some way, such as not being what was agreed on."

"But they wrote me that my design was of excellent quality."

"Great, then that takes care of that issue. How about the other one? Do you ever do preliminary work without expecting to be paid unless the deal goes through? And is that a common way to operate in your business?"

"Me? Never! I don't have to. I suppose some designers do, or at least prepare detailed proposals without pay, but I have more work than I can decently do and I make it clear to all potential clients that I charge for preliminary drawings. In this situation, as I said, we agreed on the price in advance."

"What about witnesses to that conversation?"

"Well, Jim, my partner, sat in on one of the early discussions. We hadn't agreed on the final price yet, but we weren't too far apart."

"Was it clear to Jim that you intended to charge and that Wickless knew you did?"

"Yes, absolutely."

"Great, bring Jim to court with you. Here is how I would proceed. Organize your statement as to what happened so that it takes you no longer than five minutes to present it to the judge. Bring your sketches, and most important, the sketch the Wickless people made, along with the letters they sent you, and show them to the judge. Then have your partner Jim testify to being present when money was discussed. You should have no trouble. If you're nervous about being in court, go down and check it out a few days before. It's just down at Center Street and I'm sure that if you watch for half an hour, you will be raring to go!"

NOTE: This little scenario is a simplified version of a real case. Don was given a judgment for the entire amount he requested and Wickless paid it.

C. OLD FRIENDS FALL OUT

Sadly, this is a typical story. Tom, a true artist when it comes to graphics, is a bit ingenuous when it comes to dollars and cents. Recognizing this, he never tried to prepare his tax returns, but for several years had turned all of his tax affairs over to Phillip, a local CPA. Price was discussed the first year, but after that Tom just paid Phillip's bill when the job was done. One spring, things went wrong. As usual, Tom's records weren't great, and he was late in getting them to Phillip. Phillip was busy and put Tom's tax return together without discussing it with him in detail. When Tom saw the return, he was shocked. He felt that he was being asked to pay way too much to Uncle Sam. He called Phillip and reminded him of a number of deductions that he felt had been overlooked. There was some discussion of whether Phillip should have known about these or not. At this time, Phillip complained about Tom's sloppy records and his delay in making them available, and Tom told Phillip that he thought that Phillip had done a hurried and substandard job. After some more grumpy talk back and forth, Phillip agreed to make the necessary corrections. In a week this was done and the return was again sent to Tom. While his tax liability was now less, Tom was still annoyed, feeling that not all of the oversights had been amended. Tom called Phillip again and this time they quickly got into a shouting match which ended with Phillip very reluctantly agreeing to look at the return a third time and Tom saying that he was taking his business to an accountant who could add. Tom did just that and after several modifications were made, resulting in a slightly lower tax liability, the return was filed. The second accountant stated that as he needed to check all of Phillip's work to satisfy himself that it was right, he ended up doing almost as much work as if he had started from scratch. He billed Tom for $500, saying that this was $250 less than if he had not had the benefit of Phillip's work.

Phillip billed Tom $1,200. Tom was furious and refused to pay. Phillip then sent Tom a demand letter stating that most of the problems were created by Tom's bad records, that he had made a number of changes when requested to do so and had offered to make the final changes at no additional charge. Tom replied with "I'll see you in court." Which is exactly what happened as Phillip went ahead with his suit.

Okay, now it's up to you. Imagine for a moment that you are Phillip. How would you prepare your case? Then do the same thing from Tom's point of view. In the spirit of not asking you questions I am afraid to answer myself, here is how I would proceed.

Phillip's Case

1. Phillip's first job is to write a clear, concise demand letter (see Chapter 7);

2. In court, Phillip will want to prove that he did work that was worth $1,200. Bringing copies of Tom's tax returns as well as his own work sheets is the simplest way to accomplish this. The returns should not be presented to the judge page by page, but as a package. The purpose is to indicate that a lot of work has been done, not to go into details;

3. Phillip should then testify as to his hourly rate and how many hours he worked. He should mention that more hours were required than would otherwise have been the case because Tom did not have the raw data well organized. To illustrate his point, Phillip should introduce the raw data Tom gave him into evidence (i.e., a shoebox full of messy receipts);

4. Phillip has now presented his basic case, which is simply that he was hired to do a job, he did it, and he wasn't paid. However, Phillip would be wise to go beyond this and anticipate at least some of Tom's defenses, which will almost surely involve the poor quality of the work done, as well as a claim that Phillip is simply charging too much. Therefore, were I Phillip, I would close my testimony with a statement along these lines:

"Your honor, when I finished my work my client pointed out that several deductions had been overlooked. I believed then and believe now that this was because the data he provided me with was inadequate, but I did rework the return and corrected several items that were left out. When my client told me that he felt that even the revised draft needed work, I again told him that I would work with him to make any necessary changes. It was at this point that he refused to let me see the returns and hired another accountant. In my professional opinion, very little work remained to be done at this stage — certainly nothing that couldn't be accomplished in an hour or two. Now, as to the amount charged, it took me twelve hours to reconstruct what went on in the typesetting business from the mess of incomplete and incoherent records I was given. At $40 per hour, this means that almost $500 of my bill involved work that had to be done prior to actually preparing the return. Taking into consideration the difficult circumstances, I believe I charged fairly for the work I did, and that I did my work well."

Tom's Case

Okay, so much for getting into the head of an indignant accountant. Now let's see how Tom, the upset typesetter, might defend his case.

1. Tom should begin by writing a letter of his own, rebutting Phillip's demand letter point by point (see Chapter 7). He should bring this letter to court and give it to the judge;

2. Next, Tom should testify that he refused to pay the bill because he felt that Phillip's work was so poorly done that he didn't trust Phillip to finish the job. Tom should testify as to the details of several of the points that Phillip overlooked. Thus, if Tom provided Phillip with information concerning his purchase of a new typesetting machine and Phillip forgot to claim the investment tax credit, this would be important evidence. But Tom should be careful to make his points relatively brief and understandable. He won't gain by a long and boring rehash of his entire return;

3. Now, to really make his case, Tom should present more detailed evidence that supports his claim that Phillip did his work poorly. The tax return as correctly prepared by the new accountant would be of some help, but far more valuable would be having the second accountant come to court to testify. Unfortunately, professionals are commonly reluctant to testify against one another, so this may be difficult to arrange. But Tom should at the very least be able to get a letter from the new accountant outlining the things that he found it necessary to do to change the return as prepared by Phillip;

4. Tom should also present to the court his cancelled checks paid Phillip for the last several years' returns, assuming, of course, that Phillip's previous bills were much less. For example, if Tom had been billed $400 and $500 in the two previous years, it would raise some questions as to Phillip's bill of $1,200 for the current year;

5. Tom should also present the bill from the second accountant to the court as well as his note explaining that his $500 charge was $250 less than his normal bill for the whole job.

NOTE: After (or perhaps during) Phillip's and Tom's testimony, the judge is almost certain to ask a number of questions. In addition, he or she will probably give each an opportunity to rebut the statements of the other. I don't have space to discuss how this might go in detail, but in rebuttal, generally it's important to focus on the one or two points that you think the judge has missed or is in danger of getting wrong. This is not a time to attempt to restate your entire case.

What Happened?

Phillip was given a judgment for $400. The judge didn't explain his reasoning, but apparently felt that there was some right on each side and split the difference with a little edge to Tom. This sort of decision where each side is given something is common in Small Claims Court and again illustrates the wisdom of the parties' working out their own compromise. Even if Tom and Phillip had arrived at a solution where one or the other gave up a little more than the judge ordered, there would have been a saving in time and aggravation that probably would have more than made up the difference.

22

MISCELLANEOUS CASES

By now you should have a clear idea as to how any Small Claims case can be sensibly presented. The facts of each situation will vary, but the general approach will not. Here I will discuss a few more common case types. If I haven't covered yours in detail, simply make your own outline of steps to be taken adopting the general approaches I have suggested.

A. CLOTHING (ALTERATION AND CLEANING)

Several years ago, before I started regularly attending Small Claims Court, I stopped by one morning when I had a few free moments to kill before a criminal hearing. The case being argued involved an elderly German-American gentleman with a strong accent, suing an equally aged Armenian tailor, who was also seriously uncomfortable with the English language. The dispute centered around whether a suitcoat that the tailor had made for the plaintiff should have had two or three buttons. After ten minutes of almost incomprehensible testimony, I understood little more than that the plaintiff had never owned a suit with two buttons and the tailor had never made one with three. The two men

176

ended by standing facing one another — each pulling a sleeve of the suitcoat and each yelling as loud as he could in his own language, apparently about how many buttons a suit ought to have. Much to their credit, the judge and bailiff just sat and smiled. What happened? I don't know. I was still actively practicing law then and had to bustle off to argue before another judge that my client thought that two pounds of marijuana he was carrying in a money belt was really oregano. You can probably guess how that argument ended.

While I have never seen another clothing case quite as colorful as that of the two button suit, I have been consistently surprised at how often I have encountered people in Small Claims Court, clutching an injured garment. We must indeed come to view our clothing as an extension of ourselves, because so many of us react with an indignation out of proportion to our monetary loss when some favorite item is damaged. I will never forget the morning I saw a particularly sour-looking fellow with neither word nor smile for anyone, including his obviously long-suffering wife, draw himself up to full height and wax poetic for five minutes about a four year old leather vest that a cleaner had mutilated.

Winning a significant victory in a case involving clothing is often difficult. Why? Because, while the liability is often easy to establish (i.e., the seamstress cut off the collar instead of the cuff), damages are difficult or impossible to prove in any reasonably amount for the obvious reason that used clothing has little actual market value, even though it may have cost a lot to start with or have enormous sentimental value to its owner. (Clothing cases are also discussed in Chapters 2 A and 4 C.) In theory a court can only award a plaintiff the fair market value of the damaged clothing, not its replacement cost. But because this rule of law commonly works a severe injustice in clothing cases (a $400 suit bought last week may only be worth $100 used this week), many judges tend to bend it a little in favor of the person who has suffered the loss.

They do this by allowing an amount pretty close to the original purchase price when the clothing involved was almost new, even though its fair market value for resale would be much less. Thus, the owner of a $200 dress that had been ruined by a seamstress

177

after only one wearing might recover $150. Judges are not required to take this approach, but many do. With older clothing, I have also seen some judges take a flexible approach. They do this by making a rough estimate as to the percentage of use that remains in a garment and then awarding the plaintiff this percentage of the original purchase price. Thus, if a cleaner ruined a $300 suit that had been worn for about 50% of its useful life, the plaintiff might recover $150.

Here are some hints:

• Bring the damaged clothing to court. It's hard for a tailor to say much when confronted with a coat that is two sizes too big or has three sleeves.

• Be ready to prove the original purchase price with a cancelled check, newspaper ad, credit card statement, etc.

• Be sure that the person you are suing (tailor, cleaner, seamstress, etc.) caused the problem. As noted in the example of the suede coat in Chapter 2, some problems that develop during cleaning or alterations may be the responsibility of the manufacturer.

NOTE: Cleaners particularly are prone to offer "proof" from "independent testing laboratories" that damage caused during cleaning wasn't their fault. You will want to ask: How much the cleaner paid the testing lab for the report? How many times had the same cleaner used the same testing lab before? How did the cleaner know about the testing lab (does it solicit business from cleaners)? etc.

B. DOG BITE CASES

Re-read Chapter 2 where I use several dog bite cases as examples. To review: be ready to prove the extent of the injury, the location where it occurred, time off from work without compensation, doctors' bills, etc. If the dog is mean-looking, a picture will be a great help. If the dog bite occurred off the dog owner's property, you have an excellent chance of recovery. If the attack occurred on a part of the owner's property where you had a clear right to be (the front walk or even the backyard if you were there by invitation), you also stand to win. However, if you were on a part of the dog owner's property where people would normally not go without invitation and you had no such invitation, the chances are you will lose.

In cases where one dog attacks another, there is normally no recovery unless the attacking dog entered the other's property, or the attacking dog was loose and the victim was on a leash. When two loose dogs get into a mix-up on neutral ground, there is not usually an award of damages to the loser.

C. POLICE BRUTALITY — FALSE ARREST CASES

Now and then actions against the police end up in Small Claims Court. Usually the plaintiff is an irate citizen who has tried and failed to get an attorney to represent him in a larger suit and, as a last resort, has filed for $750 in Small Claims.* Put simply, most of the people I have seen bringing this sort of case have been run out of court in a hurry. Why? Because the police and jailors have

* In most cases of this sort, you will want to sue the city, county or state government that employs the officer as well as the individual involved. In California, before you can sue a government entity, you must promptly file an administrative claim (see Chapter 8).

excellent legal advice and aren't afraid to lie to back each other up. The unwritten rule in any law enforcement agency is to protect your own derriere first, and to protect your buddies' derrieres right after that. Cops are not going to politely sit still and collect black marks on their service records without fighting back. Most law enforcement people have testified many times before and know how to handle themselves.

The reason that many plaintiffs must use Small Claims Court to sue law enforcement people pretty much tells the story. Lawyers won't normally invest their time and money in this sort of case because they find them almost impossible to win. Does this mean that I believe that people bringing false arrest, police brutality and similar type cases are wasting their time? Balancing the trouble involved, against the unlikely chance of success, I would have to say yes. That said, let me also say that I believe that lots of things that make little sense at a practical level, are worthwhile at many others. I can't help but admire people who will fight for principal, even though they have small chance of winning.

If you do sue a cop, jailor or anyone else with a badge, be sure that you have several witnesses who will back you up, and won't be intimidated into keeping their mouths shut. Never, never rely on one officer to testify against another. They simply won't do it. It may be cynical, but it is also realistic to assume that all cops will tell whatever lies necessary to protect themselves and each other. This isn't always true, but it happens often enough so that you may as well be prepared for the worst. You would also be wise to spend a few dollars and talk to a lawyer who specializes in criminal cases. For a $25-50 fee, you can probably pick up some valuable pointers as to how to convince the judge that you were treated in an illegal and unreasonable way.

D. DAMAGE TO REAL PROPERTY (LAND, BUILDINGS, ETC.)

There is no typical case of this nature, as facts vary greatly. So instead of trying to set down general rules, let's look at a situation that happened recently to a friend of mine. (Let's call her Babette.)

Babette owns a cinder-block building that houses two stores. One morning when she came to work, she noticed water pouring in through the back of her building. Because the building was set into a hill, it abutted about eight feet of her uphill neighbor's land. (Let's call her neighbor Boris). After three days of investigation involving the use of green dye in Boris's plumbing system, it was discovered that the water came from an underground leak in Boris's sewer pipe. At this point, Babette had spent considerable effort and some money to pay helpers to get the water mopped up before it damaged anything in the stores.

Instead of fixing the leak promptly, Boris delayed for four days. All of this time, Babette and her helpers were mopping frantically. Finally, when Boris did get to work, he insisted on digging the pipe out himself, which took another four days. (A plumber with the right equipment could have done it in one.) In the middle of Boris's digging, when his yard looked as though it was being attacked by a herd of giant gophers, it rained. The water filled the holes and trenches instead of running off as it normally would have. Much of it ran through the ground into Babette's building.

When the flood was finally over, Babette figured out her costs as follows:

First three days (before the source of the water was discovered)	$148 (for help with mopping)
Next four days (while Boris refused to cooperate)	$288 (for help with mopping)
Final four days (including day it rained)	$262 (for help with mopping)
One secondhand water vacuum purchased during rain storm	$200
Her own time, valued at $7.00 per hour	$500

Assuming that Boris is unwilling to pay Babette's costs, for what amount should she sue and how much is she likely to recover? If you remember the lessons taught in Chapter 2, you will remember that before Babette can recover for her very real loss, she must show that Boris was negligent or caused her loss intentionally. Probably, she can't do this for the first three days, when no one knew where the water was coming from. However, once the problem was discovered and Boris didn't take immediate steps to fix it, he was clearly negligent, and she can recover at least her out-of-pocket loss ($550 for labor and $200 for the water vacuum). Can Babette also recover for the value of her own time? The answer to this question is *maybe*. If she could show that she had to close her store or take time off from a job to stem the flood, she probably could recover. Were I she, I would sue for the Small Claims maximum and count on getting all, or most, of it.

23

JUDGMENT AND APPEAL

A. THE JUDGMENT

The decision in your case will be mailed to the address on record with the clerk any time from a few days to a few weeks after your case is heard. The exception to this rule is when one side doesn't show up and the other wins by default. Default judgments are normally announced right in the courtroom.* The truth is that in the vast majority of contested cases the judge has already made up his/her mind at the time your case is heard and notes down his/her decision before you leave the courtroom. Decisions are sent by mail because the court doesn't want to deal with angry, unhappy losers, especially those few who might get violent. As one bailiff recently put it, "The county simply can't afford to clean the blood off the floor every time the loser goes after the winner or the judge". As you might guess, judges are particularly concerned about the latter possibility.

---

* In Chapters 10, 12 and 15, we discuss default judgments and the fact that people who have had defaults entered against them can often get them set aside if (1) they had a decent excuse for not being present, and (2) they notify the court clerk immediately of their desire to have the judgment set aside.

Often when a judgment is entered against a person, he or she feels that the judge would surely have made a different decision if he or she hadn't gotten mixed up, or overlooked some crucial fact, or had properly understood an argument. On the basis of my experience on the bench, I can tell you that in the vast majority of Small Claims cases, there is little likelihood that the judge would change his or her decision even if you had a chance to argue the whole case over. In any event, you don't. You have had your chance and the decision has gone against you. Don't call the judge, or go see him, or send him documents through the mail. You had your chance in court, you don't get another chance in the judge's office (see D, below for appeal rights).

NOTE: Now that a judgment has been entered, we need to expand our vocabulary slightly. The person who wins the case (gets the judgment) now becomes "the judgment creditor" and the loser is known as "the judgment debtor".

B. TIME PAYMENTS

We have mentioned the fact that in California a judge may order that the loser be allowed to pay the winner over a period of time, rather than all at once. The judge won't normally make this sort of order unless you request it. So, if you have no real defense to a claim, or if you have a fairly good case but aren't sure which way the judge will go, be sure that the judge knows that, if the judgment goes against you, you wish to have time to pay. You might put your request this way:

•"In closing my presentation, I would like to say that I believe I have a convincing case and should be awarded the judgment, but in the event that you rule for my opponent, I would like you to allow me time payments of no more than (whatever amount is convenient) per month."

Or, if you have no real defense:

•"Your Honor, I request that you enter the judgment against me for no more than (an amount convenient to you) per month."

If you neglect to ask for time payments in court and wish to make this request after you receive the judgment, first contact the other party to see if he will voluntarily agree to accept his money on a schedule you can afford to pay. If he or she agrees, it would be wise to write your agreement down and each sign it. If your opponent is an all-or-nothing sort of person and refuses payments, promptly contact the court clerk and ask that the case again be brought before the judge — not as to the facts, but only to set up a payment schedule that you can live with.

```
 1
 2
 3          SMALL CLAIMS COURT, FOR _____
 4          JUDICIAL DISTRICT, COUNTY OF _____, STATE OF CALIFORNIA
 5
 6   JOHN TOLLER,                    )
 7              Plaintiff           )        Action Number SC._____
 8   v.                             )
 9   MILDRED EDWARDS,               )        PETITION, NOTICE OF MOTION,
                                    )        AND ORDER ALLOWING JUDGMENT TO BE
10              Defendant.          )        PAID IN INSTALLMENTS.
11   _____
12          Comes now MILDRED EDWARDS and represents to the court that a judgment was
13   entered against her in the above entitled action in the amount of $526.00.  That
14   payment of this entire judgment immediately will cause a severe hardship to
15   MILDRED EDWARDS because ___(of lack of employment, or illness or whatever)___.
16   Petitioner can pay $25.00 per month.
17          Wherefore petitioner requests that an order by made to allow payment in
18   this amount.
19
20   DATED:_____            _____
21                                            PETITIONER
22                         NOTICE OF MOTION
23          To JOHN TOLLER.  Please take note that you are ordered to appear in court
24   on ___(date)_____ at ___(time)_____ to give any legal reason why
25   it shall not be ordered that the judgment in the above entitled case be paid in
26   installments of $25.00 per month.
27
28   DATED:_____    _____
                                              JUDGE
```

```
 1                              ORDER
 2        Judgment to be paid $25.00 on the first day of each month until fully
 3   paid.  Should the judgment debtor fail to make one or more payments the judgment
 4   creditor may file an affidavit so stating with this court and the above order
 5   shall thereby be vacated and the clerk shall proceed as if it had not been made.
 6
 7   DATED:_____              _____
 8                                            JUDGE
 9
10
11
12
13
14
15
16
17
18
19
20
21
22
23
24
25
26
27
28
```

C. SATISFACTION OF JUDGMENT

Here is a sample "Satisfaction of Judgment" form which is available from the Small Claims Court clerk. It must be signed by the judgment creditor. It is a good idea to get the satisfaction form filled out and signed when you pay the judgment. This saves the trouble of having to track down the other party later. Besides, people are much more willing to be cooperative when you are waving money under their nose than when they have already spent it. Once signed, you file the Satisfaction of Judgment with the Small Claims Court clerk. This clerk can give you a certified copy of the satisfaction if you ever need one.

```
211 190

              SMALL CLAIMS COURT, BERKELEY-ALBANY JUDICIAL DISTRICT,
                      COUNTY OF ALAMEDA, STATE OF CALIFORNIA


     _____        NO. SC _____
                    Plaintiff(s)
              vs                             SATISFACTION OF JUDGMENT

     _____
                    Defendant(s)


     I hereby acknowledge full satisfaction of the judgment in the above entitled action.

     Executed at _____ . California on _____


                                             _____
                                                          Judgment Creditor
```

1. The Right to a "Satisfaction of Judgment"

The law states that a "judgment creditor" must file a "satisfaction of judgment" form with the court when he or she is paid (Code of Civil Procedure Section 117.9). If a judgment creditor who receives payment in full on a judgment fails to do this, the judgment debtor should send a written demand that this be done. A first class letter is adequate. If, after written demand, the judgment creditor still doesn't file his satisfaction without just cause, the judgment debtor is entitled to recover all actual damages he or she may sustain by reason of such failure and, in addition, shall be awarded $50 by way of punitive damages.

2. Getting A "Satisfaction Of Judgment" From A Person You Can't Find

Sometimes people forget to get a "Satisfaction of Judgment" when they pay a judgment, only to find later that they can't locate the judgment creditor. If this happens, consult the court clerk.

187

You will have to prepare an affidavit as to your unsuccessful attempt to find the judgment creditor and submit it to the court with your proof that the judgment was paid.

D. THE APPEAL

If, in the face of justice, common sense and all of your fine arguments, the judge turns out to be a big dummy and rules for your opponent, you can appeal to a higher court, right? Not necessarily. In Small Claims Court if you are the person who brought the suit (the plaintiff) and you lose, you are finished, done, through. Plaintiffs have absolutely no right to appeal anywhere. Why? Because that's how the legislature made the rules. However, if you are the defendant and lose, you can appeal to the Superior Court if, and only if, you do it promptly.

Isn't it unfair, maybe even unconstitutional, to allow appeal rights for defendants and none for plaintiffs? I will leave it to you to decide the fairness issue, but it's not unconstitutional for the simple reason that a plaintiff knows before he files that he doesn't have a right to an appeal. He has a choice of bringing his suit in Small Claims Court where there is no right for plaintiffs to appeal, or in Municipal Court where both sides can appeal. The defendant doesn't have this opportunity to pick the court and, therefore, the legislature decided that his or her appeal rights should be preserved.

E. FILING YOUR APPEAL

Now let's look at the mechanics of the appeal. In California, the defendant must file a notice of appeal within 20 days of the entry of the judgment. As judgments are mailed, this means that there will be less than 20 days to file an appeal from the day that the defendant receives the judgment. The date the judgment was entered will appear on the judgment. If for some reason attributable to the magic of the U.S. Postal Service your judgment doesn't show up within 20 days after it was entered, call the Small Claims clerk immediately and request help in getting an extension of time to file your appeal.

To file your notice of appeal, go to the Small Claims clerk's office and fill out a paper such as the one illustrated below. Currently, the appeal fee is close to $25. You are now going into Superior Court and you must pay according to their fee schedule. There is no charge for the original plaintiff to appear in Superior Court on an appeal. Indeed, if the Small Claims judgment is affirmed in whole or in part or the appeal is dismissed, the defendant shall not only be ordered to pay the amount of the judgment, but also interest, costs and the sum of $15 as an attorney fee.

<table>
<tr><td>NOTICE OF APPEAL
AND NOTICE OF
FILING APPEAL</td><td>IN THE SMALL CLAIMS DIVISION
.... JUDICIAL DISTRICT
COUNTY OF LOS ANGELES, STATE OF CALIFORNIA</td><td>Case Number
(Fill in number)</td></tr>
</table>

.... John Albertson .... v. .... Gloria Ferdinand ....

Plaintiff(s)   Defendant(s)

Appellant (Name and address):

    Gloria Ferdinand
    66 Echo St. Apt A
    Los Angeles, CA

Appellant (Name and address of each):

Respondent (Name and Address):

    John Albertson
    106 Easy Way
    Inglewood, CA

The undersigned appeals from the judgment of the small claims division of this court to the superior court.

Dated:......(Date)..: _____Gloria Ferdinand_____

                                                 Signature of Apellant

NOTICE OF FILING NOTICE OF APPEAL

TO:
  Above-named
Respondent(s)

    Notice of Appeal was filed in this court on (date)..

Dated: .... By _____ Deputy Clerk

Do not contact the Court regarding the Appeal. You will be notified by the Superior Court of the Case Number and date set for trial

CLERK'S CERTIFICATE OF MAILING

I certify that I am not a party to this cause and that a copy of the foregoing was mailed first class, postage prepaid,

at (Place): ....

California in a sealed envelope addressed to Respondent(s) as shown above, and that the mailing of the foregoing

and execution of this certificate occurred on (Date): ....

                            Clerk of the above-named Court

                            By_____, Deputy

NOTICE OF APPEAL AND NOTICE OF FILING APPEAL

76N592D-SC 16-(6)-PS 12-76   116; 117.8; 117.10; 118.1; 1013a(3) CCP
                                           CRC 152(a) (c)

When you file your appeal, the court will notify the other side that you have done so. You need not do this yourself. Once your appeal is on file at the Superior Court, your next step is to wait. When you are done waiting, you will probably have to wait some more. You are in the formal court system now, where traditionally very little happens, very slowly. Those who have been in the armed services will understand. All the deadlines apply to you — never to the bureaucracy. Eventually (two to six months depending on the county) you will get a notice giving you a court date in the Superior Court.*

F. ARGUING YOUR APPEAL

You are entitled to have an attorney in Superior Court. But as your case is not worth a lot, you will probably decide that it is not wise to hire one. Indeed there should be little practical reason for an attorney, as you probably have an excellent grasp of the issues by this time. However, it's often true that judges pay more attention to the same argument made by an attorney than made by an ordinary citizen. I find this to be yet another manifestation of the sickness of our judicial system but you are stuck dealing with the system as it is, not as it should be.

An appeal of a Small Claims judgment is not the sort ot appeal that the U.S. Supreme Court hears. The Supreme Court, and the other formal appellate courts, are concerned with looking at the written record of what went on in a lower court with the idea of changing a decision when a judge has misinterpreted the law. Since no record has been made in Small Claims Court, the Superior Court has nothing to look over. They must start from scratch, as if nothing had been said in Small Claims Court. You simply argue the case over, presenting all your witnesses, documents, etc. Of course, both sides should give some thought to how their presentation can be improved. This is particularly true of the defendant, who has already lost once.

Oh, and something else. You are now in a court where formal

---

* Remember, in Chapter 20 I said that landlords can get into real trouble if a defendant appeals an eviction order. This is because the tenant can stay in the unit while the appeal is pending. This rule needs to be changed, or appeals must be greatly speeded up.

trappings, rules and language are in vogue. Chances are the judge will be lenient with you, but you may find that you feel a little like a puppy dropped onto a freeway. The best cure for this sense of panic is to go watch a few Small Claims appeals for a day or two before you case is scheduled. Simply ask the Superior Court clerk to tell you when they are scheduled. If you are going to bother to appeal your case, you may as well do your homework.

24

COLLECTING YOUR MONEY

OK, you won, what does that mean? Simply that you are entitled to the dollar amount of the judgment from the opposing party or parties. How are you going to get it? Try asking politely. This works in the majority of cases, especially if you have sued a respectable business. If you don't have personal contact with the person who owes you the money, try a note. Plaintiffs should wait 20 days after the day the judgment is entered before trying to collect. If you make your request for money too soon, you may remind the defendant to take advantage of his right to appeal.

If you receive no response to your polite note, you will have to get serious about collecting your money or forget it. The emphasis in the previous sentence is on the word "you". Much to many people's surprise, the court does not enforce its judgments and collect money for you — you have to do it yourself.

There are only a few relatively easy ways to collect money from a debtor. We mentioned these briefly in Chapter 3. Hopefully you gave some thought to collection before you brought your case. If you only now realize that your opponent doesn't have the money to buy a toothbrush and never will, you are better off not wasting

```
┌─────────────────────────────────────────────────────────────┐
│                                                               │
│                  SAMPLE COLLECTION NOTE                       │
│                                                               │
│                            P.O. Box 66                        │
│                            Berkeley, Calif.                   │
│                                                               │
│                            February 15, 19___                 │
│                                                               │
│       Mildred Edwards                                         │
│       11 Milvia Street                                        │
│       Berkeley, Calif. 94706                                  │
│                                                               │
│       Dear Mrs. Edwards:                                      │
│                                                               │
│           As you know, a judgment was entered against you in  │
│       Small Claims Court on January 15 in the amount of       │
│       $457.86.  As the judgment creditor I will appreciate    │
│       your paying this amount at your earliest convenience.   │
│                                                               │
│       Thank you for your consideration.                       │
│                            Very truly yours,                  │
│                                                               │
│                                                               │
│                            John Toller                        │
│                                                               │
└─────────────────────────────────────────────────────────────┘
```

more time and money trying to get him to pay up. Also, remember that a judgment is valid for ten years and can be renewed for an additional ten if you can show that you have tried to collect it, but failed. In some situations you may simply want to sit on it, with the hope that your "judgment debtor" will show a few signs of life in the future.

A. LEVYING ON WAGES, BANK ACCOUNTS, BUSINESS ASSETS, REAL PROPERTY, ETC.

If a polite letter doesn't work (two weeks is plenty of time to wait), and you know that the person who owes you the money (the "judgment debtor") has it, you will have to start acting like a collection agency.*

If you know where the judgment debtor works, you are in good shape. Federal and state law allow you to get approximately 25% of a person's net wages to satisfy a debt.** Knowing where a

---

* It is possible to turn your debt over to a real collection agency, but this probably doesn't make too much sense as the agency will take 50% of what they can collect. Unless you are a regular customer, the agency probably won't treat your debt with much priority unless they believe that it is easy to collect. If it is easy for them to collect, it probably won't be hard for you to do it yourself and save the fee.
** If a person has a very low income, the amount you can recover can be considerably less than 25%.

judgment debtor banks can also be extremely valuable as you can order a sheriff or marshal to levy on a bank account and get whatever it contains at the time of the levy. Of course, a bank account levy will only work once as the debtor is pretty sure to move his account when he realizes that you have emptied it. Other types of property are normally much more difficult to grab. Why? Because California has a number of "exemption" laws which say that, even though a person owes money, certain types of his/her property can't be taken to satisfy the debt. Items protected include a family house with $30,000 in equity, furniture, clothes, and much more. Practically speaking, the only assets other than wages and bank accounts that are normally worth thinking about to satisfy a Small Claims judgment are motor vehicles in which the judgment debtor has an equity of more than $500, real property other than the place where the debtor lives, and the receipts of an operating business. Theoretically, there are many other assets that you could reach, but in most cases they are not worth the time and expense involved, considering that your judgment is for the Small Claims maximum, or less.*

1. The Writ Of Execution

Before you can levy on a person's wages or other property, you need to get a court order called a "Writ of Execution". If you have a Small Claims judgment, you are entitled to this writ. You get your Writ from the Small Claims Court clerk who will help you fill it out. The charge is $1.50, which is a recoverable cost (see C below).

2. The Sheriff (Or Marshal)

Once your "Writ of Execution" form is filled out, take or send it to the sheriff or marshal in the county where the assets are located. The Small Claims Court clerk will do this for you if you request that they do so. Do it right away, as the Writ of Execution expires in 60 days if it is not served by the sheriff or marshal. If this time runs out, you will have to go back to the Small Claims clerk

---

* You will find a complete list of exempt property and a thorough discussion of debtors' rights including bankruptcy in *The California Debtors' Handbook – Bill Payers' Rights*, Warner and Honigsberg, Nolo Press.

170-030 (jc79)

NAME AND ADDRESS OF ATTORNEY	TELEPHONE	FOR COURT USE ONLY
John Toller P.O. Box 66 Berkeley, CA 94702	(415) 845-0000	

ATTORNEY FOR (Name)

Insert name of court, judicial district or branch court, if any, and post office and street address.

(fill in court)

PLAINTIFF	CASE NUMBER
John Toller	

	FOR RECORDER'S USE ONLY
DEFENDANT Mildred Edwards	

WRIT OF EXECUTION ☒MONEY JUDGMENT ☐POSSESSION OF ☐REAL ☐JOINT DEBTOR ☐PERSONAL PROPERTY

(fill in county

1. To the Sheriff or any Marshal or Constable of the County of   where assets are located)
You are directed to satisfy the judgment described below, with interest and costs and your costs and disbursements. as provided by law. This writ may not be used for a levying officer's sale of a dwelling house as defined in CCP 690 31.

2. To any registered process server: You are authorized to serve this writ only, in accord with CCP 687.

3. Judgment creditor (Name):

   John Toller

4. Judgment debtor (Name and address):
☐ Additional name and address on reverse.

   Mildred Edwards

5. Judgment entered on (Date):

(the clerk will supply this information)

6. Notice of sale under this writ ☐ has not been requested ☐ has been requested as set forth on the reverse.

7. ☐ Joint debtor information set forth on the reverse.

8. ☐ Real or personal property described on the reverse

(SEAL)

9. Total judgment as entered
  a. Principal: . . . . $
  b. Attorney fees: . . . . $
  c. Interest: . . . . $
  d. Costs: . . . . $ _____
  e. Total (Add 9a,b,c,d): . . . . $
10. Total judgment and accruals
  a. Interest (On item 9e) as adjusted for payments and partial satisfactions (Per filed affidavit CCP 682.2): . . . . $
  b. Costs (Per filed memo of costs after judgment): . . . . . . $
  c. Total (Add 9e,10a,b). . . . . $
11. Net balance due on judgment
  a. Payments and partial satisfactions. . . . . $
  b. Net balance due before issuance of writ (Subtract 11a from 10c): $
  c. Fee for issuance of writ . . . . . $ _____
  d. Net balance due on date of writ (Add 11b,c) . . . . $
12. Levying officer: Add the following daily interest from date of writ to date of levy (7% per year on 9e or 11b, whichever is less). . . . . $

(fill in the correct amounts)

Dated: Clerk, By _____, Deputy

NOTICE TO JUDGMENT DEBTOR: SEE REVERSE FOR IMPORTANT INFORMATION

(Continued on reverse)

Do NOT use this form for levy and sale of a dwelling house as defined in CCP 690 31 The singular includes the plural

Form Approved by the
Judicial Council of California
Revised Effective January 1 1979   **WRIT OF EXECUTION**   15 USC §1673, CCP 681 et seq.
690 1 et seq, 690 50, 692a.
989-994, 1032 6, 1033 et seq

and get another "Writ of Execution" issued. Give the sheriff (marshal) or Small Claims clerk:

a. The "Writ of Execution" (original) and one to three or more copies depending on the asset to be collected; *

b. His fees for collecting (this will vary as to the type of asset, so you should inquire);

---

* Don't forget to keep a copy of the "Writ of Execution" for your files.

c. Instructions on what and where to collect. The sheriff, marshal or Small Claims clerk may have a form they wish you to use when giving them instructions. Ask about the fee when you call. Normally a letter is sufficient.

3. How To Levy On Wages And Bank Accounts

To seize a person's wages or bank account you need the original and one copy of a "Writ of Execution", $8.50 for the sheriff (marshal) fee, and a letter of instruction:

```
                              P.O. Box 66
                              Berkeley, Calif.

                              March 1, 19___

Sheriff (Civil Division), Alameda County
Alameda County Courthouse
Oakland, California
                              Re: John Toller v. Mildred Edwards
                                  Albany-Berkeley Judicial Dist-
                                  rict
                                  Small Claims Court No. 81-52
Dear Sir:

    Enclosed you will find the original and one copy of a Writ of Execu-
tion issued by the Small Claims Court for the Oakland Judicial District
in the amount of $___(fill in total due)___.  I also enclose a check
for your fee in the amount of $_____.

    I hereby instruct you to levy on the wages of Mildred Edwards, who
works at the Graphite Oil Co., 1341 Chester St., Oakland, Calif.  Please
serve the Writ on or before March 15, 19___.*


                              Very truly yours,


                              John Toller
```

4. Levying On Motor Vehicles (Including Planes, Boats And R.V.s)

Getting money from wages or bank accounts is fairly easy. Selling a person's motor vehicle is more difficult for several reasons, including the following.

---

* For a bank account, you would simply substitute "all monies in the checking account of Mildred Edwards, located at the Bank of Trade, 11 City St., Oakland, Ca." Where a bank account is in the name of defendant and someone else, you will have to post a bond for twice the amount in the account to levy. Ask the sheriff or marshal for details.

a. $500 in equity in a car is exempt from your levy (California Code of Civil Procedure 690.2).

EXAMPLE: A judgment debtor has a car worth $1,500 on which he owes $1,000. This means that his equity is $500 — the bank owns the rest. As an equity of $500 is exempt under C.C.P. 690.2, you would end up with nothing.

b. A motor vehicle is exempt from attachment up to $2,500 if it is a "tool of a person's trade" (California Code of Civil Procedure 690.4).

EXAMPLE: A "judgment debtor" has a pickup truck worth $2,000 which she uses every day in her gardening business. The truck would be exempt under C.C.P. 690.4.

c. The judgment debtor may not own the car he drives. It may be in someone else's name, or he may owe a bank or finance company as much or more than the car is worth.

To find out if a judgment debtor owns the car he drives, go to the Department of Motor Vehicles and give them the license number. For a small fee, they will tell you who owns the car, including whether or not a bank or finance company is involved. Once you have this information, you can determine whether it is worthwhile to have the sheriff pick up the car and sell it. Levying on motor vehicles can be expensive. The storage fees and the sheriff's cost ot sale average about $175 and must be paid in advance. This money is recoverable when the vehicle is sold. Call the sheriff or marshal (Civil Division) of the county in which the car is located to find out how much money he requires as a deposit with your Writ of Execution and how many copies of the Writ you need. Then write the following letter:

```
                                    P.O. Box 66
                                    Berkeley, Calif.

                                    March 1, 19___


Sheriff (Civil Division)
Alameda County
Alameda County Courthouse
Oakland, California
                                    Re: John Toller v. Mildred Edwards
                                        Small Claims Court
                                        Albany-Berkeley Judicial Dist-
                                        rict
                                        No. SC 81-52
Dear Sir:

    You are hereby instructed, under the authority of the enclosed Writ
of Execution, to levy upon and sell all of the right, title and inter-
est of Mildred Edwards, judgment debtor, in the following motor vehicle:
```

```
(Type here all information regarding the description of the
  car from your D.M.V. report, including the license number.)

The vehicle is registered in the name(s) of Mildred Edwards and is
regularly found at the following address(es):

(List home and work address of owner)

Enclosed is my check for $_____ to cover your costs of levy and
sale.


                              Very truly yours,



                              John Toller
```

5. Real Property

It normally makes little sense to go through the complicated procedures involved in selling, or trying to sell, a person's real property to satisfy a Small Claims judgment — especially when the simple act of recording an "Abstract of Judgment" at the County Recorder's office in any (or all) counties where the judgment debtor owns real property gives you a lien against all of his real property in that county. When the judgment debtor wishes to sell his real property, the title will be clouded by your lien and he will have to pay you off to be able to transfer clear title to a third party. Thus, sooner or later, you will get your money.

To record your judgment against real property, first get an "Abstract of Judgment" from the Small Claims clerk's office. The clerk will prepare this paper for you for $1.50. Then take the "Abstract of Judgment" to the County Recorder's office in the county where the property is located, pay a $7.00 fee and give the Recorder the mailing address of the judgment debtor so that they can be notified. They will do the rest.

6. Other Personal Property

Normally, it isn't worth the trouble to try to levy on small items of personal property such as furniture or appliances because they are commonly covered by one or another of the state exemption

---

* The only exception to this rule is that a home on which the judgment debtor has filed a homestead prior to your filing your "Abstract of Judgment" can be sold and the money (up to $45,000 in equity for a family, the blind or single persons over 65, and $30,000 for a single person under 65) used to buy another homesteaded home within six months without paying off your lien. If you wish information as to how to fill out the simple form necessary to homestead your house, see *Protect Your Home With A Declaration of Homestead*, Warner, Sherman and Ihara, Nolo Press.

laws which state that certain possessions are exempt from being taken to satisfy debts. The exemption laws are found listed in C.C.P. Section 690 and include furniture, clothing, a cheap car and much more.

7. Business Assets

It is possible to have someone from the sheriff or marshal's office sent to the business of a person who owes you money to collect it from the cash on hand. This can be done in three ways as follows:

a. Till Tap: A deputy goes to the business one time and picks up all the money in the till. The fee for this service varies from $10-$35 depending on the county.

b. Eight Hour Keeper: A deputy stays all day at the place of business and collects all the money that comes in. Average fee — $35-$70.

c. 48 Hour Keeper: The deputy stays at the business for a much longer period of time and collects what comes in. Average fee — $200-$350 depending on the county.

Talk to the sheriff or marshal in your area to get more details. They will want an original and three copies of your Writ of Execution as well as instructions telling them where and when to go.

8. Pensions And Retirement Benefits

You can get at money in individual or self-employment retirement plans held in any bank or savings institution. You go after
this money just as you do any other money kept in a bank. Of
course, you need to know where the money is.

Private company retirement plans and state or local government
retirement plans can't be touched until the money is paid over to
the employee.

Federal government payroll checks and pension and retirement
benefits may not be garnisheed to satisfy any debts, except those
for alimony and child support.

B. FINDING PHANTOM ASSETS — THE JUDGMENT DEBTOR'S STATEMENT

As you now understand from reading the above section, collecting money isn't difficult if the judgment creditor has some and
you know where it is. But what do you do when you know only
that the money exists, but have no idea how to find it? For example, you may know that a person works, but not where, or that he
has money in the bank, but not which one. Wouldn't it be nice to
simply ask the judgment debtor a few questions which he had to
answer?

Well, thanks to California Code of Civil Procedure Section 117.19(b), you can do just that. Here's how it works. When a Small Claims Court judgment is entered against a person (or business) the loser must fill out a form entitled the Judgment Debtor's Statement of Assets. This form must be sent to the person who won the case within 35 days after Notice of Entry of Judgment is mailed out by the clerk *unless* the loser pays off the judgment, appeals or makes a motion to vacate the judgment. If the defendant appeals or files a motion to vacate and subsequently loses, he or she has 30 days to pay or fill out the Judgment Debtor's Statement.

. . . . COURT, SMALL CLAIMS DIVISION
. . . . COURT DISTRICT
(Address and Telephone Number of Court)
. . . . COUNTY, CALIFORNIA

SMALL CLAIM CASE NO

PLAINTIFF (Name and address)

DEFENDANT (Name and address of each)

JUDGMENT DEBTOR'S STATEMENT OF ASSETS

The *judgment debtor* in this small claims case is the person (or business) who lost the case and owes money to the winner. The winner of the case is the *judgment creditor.*

TO THE JUDGMENT DEBTOR:

The small claims court has decided you owe money to the judgment creditor

1 Unless you pay, appeal or move to vacate, you must fill out this form and send it to the person who won the case within **35 days** after the Notice of Entry of Judgment is mailed to you by the clerk

2 If you file an appeal or a Motion to Vacate, you do not need to fill out this form unless you lose your appeal or motion to vacate Then you will have 30 days to pay or complete this form and deliver it to the judgment creditor IF YOU FAIL TO DO SO YOU MAY HAVE TO GO TO COURT TO ANSWER QUESTIONS OR THE COURT CAN IMPOSE PENALTIES ON YOU

If you were sued as an individual skip this box and begin with no. 1 below Otherwise, check the applicable box, attach the documents indicated and complete no 12 on the reverse

a. ☐ (Corporation or partnership) Attached to this form is a statement describing the nature, value and exact location of all assets of the corporation or the partners, and a statement showing that the person signing this form is authorized to submit this form on behalf of the corporation or partnership

b. ☐ (Governmental agency) Attached to this form is the statement of an authorized representative of the agency as to when the agency will pay the judgment and any reasons for its failure to do so

EMPLOYMENT

1. What is your occupation?

2. Name and address of your business or employer

3. How often are you paid?
a. ☐daily ☐weekly ☐every two weeks ☐twice a month ☐monthly ☐other *(explain)*

4. What is your gross pay each pay period? $ . . . .

5. What is your take home pay each pay period? $ . . . .

6. If your wife or husband earns any income give the name and address of the business or employer:

(Continued on reverse)

Form approved by the Judicial Council of California Effective January 1, 1981 SC-133(81)

JUDGMENT DEBTOR'S STATEMENT OF ASSETS (SMALL CLAIMS)

Code of Civil Procedure § 117 19(b)

CASH, BANK DEPOSITS

7. How much money do you have in cash? $

8. How much other money do you have in banks, savings and loans, credit unions and other
financial institutions either in your own name or jointly (list):

Name and address of financial institution	Account number	Individual or joint?	Balance
a.			$
b.			$
c.			$

PROPERTY

9. List all automobiles, other vehicles and boats owned in your name or jointly:

Make and year	Value	Legal owner if different from registered owner	Amount owed
a.	$		$
b.	$		$
c.	$		$
d.	$		$

10. List all real estate owned in your name or jointly

Address of real estate	Fair market value	Amount owed
a.	$	$
b.	$	$

OTHER PERSONAL PROPERTY [*Do not list household furniture and furnishings, appliances, or clothing.*]

11. List anything of value not listed above owned in your name or jointly

Description	Value	Address where property is located
a.	$	
b.	$	
c.	$	
d.	$	
e.	$	
f.	$	
g.	$	
h.	$	
i.	$	
j.	$	

12. I declare under penalty of perjury under the laws of the State of California that the foregoing, including any attachments, is true and correct and that this declaration is executed on (date)
at (place)

. . . .

(Type or print name)   (Signature)

Mail or deliver this completed form to the judgment creditor at the address shown on the Notice of Entry of Judgment form.

WARNING! Judgment debtors who don't fill out the form may be held in contempt of court which means that a fine or, in theory, even a sentence of a few days in jail could be imposed.

WINNER'S NOTE: If you won your Small Claims Court case, have not been paid and no appeal has been filed, you are entitled to receive the Judgment Debtor's Statement of Assets form. If you don't receive this form within 35 days from the day the clerk mails you the notice that you won the case *or* if you do get the form and the judgment debtor hasn't filled it out in good faith, see the Small Claims Court clerk and ask that procedures be instituted to require that the judgment debtor appear before a judge.

C. RECOVERING COLLECTION COSTS AND INTEREST

Costs incurred prior to recovering a judgment should be included in the judgment total. I discuss this in Chapter 15 C.

Here I am concerned with costs incurred after judgment. These are the costs that result when the judgment debtor doesn't pay voluntarily and you have had to levy on his or her assets. This can be expensive and you will want to make the judgment debtor pay, if possible. Many costs of collecting a judgment are recoverable, some are not. Generally speaking, you can recover your direct costs of collecting which include such things as sheriff fees, fees to get papers (i.e., "Writ of Execution", "Abstract of Judgment") issued, and recording fees. You can also recover interest on the judgment at a rate of 7% per year. Indirect costs such as babysitting costs, time off from work, postage, gasoline, etc., can't be recovered.

There are two principal ways to collect your costs:

1. Writ Of Execution

If you will turn back a few pages to the sample "Writ of Execution" you will see that as part of levying on wages, bank accounts, automobiles, businesses, etc. collection fees can simply be added to the total to be collected. These include the fee for issuing the Writ of Execution and the sheriff's fee for collecting it. This can really add up as the sheriff's fees for selling a motor vehicle, or placing a keeper at a place of business are considerable. In addition, you can collect any interest that has accrued on the original judgment.

2. Memorandum Of Credits, Accrued Interest And Costs After Judgment

Other costs, such as money expended for an "Abstract of Judgment", County Recorder fees and costs for unsuccessful levies on wages, bank accounts, businesses or motor vehicles can be recovered only after court approval. To get these you must file a "Memorandum of Credits, Accrued Interest and Costs After Judgment". The Small Claims Court clerk will help you prepare this form. File one copy with the clerk and have a friend mail another copy to the judgment debtor. Then have your friend fill out a "Proof of Service" (see Chapter 11 F) to be filed with the clerk.

Name, Address and Telephone No. of Attorney(s)

Space Below for Use of Court Clerk Only

Peter Plaintiff
123 Broadway
Albany, CA

848-7938

Attorney(s) for   IN PRO PER

MUNICIPAL COURT OF CALIFORNIA, COUNTY OF ALAMEDA

BERKELEY-ALBANY JUDICIAL DISTRICT

Peter Plaintiff

Plaintiff(s) vs

Doris Defendant

Defendant(s)

(Abbreviated Title)

CASE NUMBER
(Fill in number)

MEMORANDUM OF CREDITS,
ACCRUED INTEREST AND
COSTS AFTER JUDGMENT

MEMORANDUM OF CREDITS

CREDIT for payments and partial satisfaction of judgment, including direct payments and executions partially satisfied: $ _____
(if none, state none)

INTEREST ACCRUED AFTER JUDGMENT

INTEREST ACCRUED AFTER JUDGMENT at 7% from date of entry of judgment on balance due after dates of payments or credits acknowledged above: $ _____

MEMORANDUM OF COSTS AFTER JUDGMENT

1 Costs after judgment claimed on memorandum filed heretofore . . . . $ _____
2 Clerk's fees . . . . $ _____
3 _____
4 Sheriff's, marshal's or constable's fees . . . . $ _____
5 _____
6 Serving supplementary proceedings . . . . $ _____
7 _____
8 Notary fees . . . . $ _____
9 _____
10 _____

TOTAL $ _____

I am the _____ of the party(s) who claim(s) these costs

To the best of my knowledge and belief the foregoing items of cost are correct and have been necessarily incurred in this action

I declare under penalty of perjury that the foregoing is true and correct.

Executed on _____ at _____, California.
(Place)

_____
(Signature of Declarant)

_____
(Type or Print Name of Declarant)

NOTE: A notice of motion to tax costs shall specify the items of the cost bill to which objection is made.
(See reverse side for Declaration of Service and Acknowledgment of Service)

**MEMORANDUM OF CREDITS, ACCRUED INTEREST
AND COSTS AFTER JUDGMENT**   C.C.P. Secs. 682.2, 1033.7, 2015.5

25

WHERE DO WE GO FROM HERE?

It's easy to criticize the existing legal system — almost everyone knows that it's on the rocks. The $350 a day experts with their degrees, titles and well-funded consulting companies have studied the problem to death with no positive results. And this is hardly surprising, since most of the experts involved in the studies and in the resulting decisions are lawyers who, at bottom, are unable to understand a problem of which they are so thoroughly a part.*

But instead of my lecturing you about all the things that are wrong at the local courthouse, let's sit down at the kitchen table with a pot of tea and a bowl of raspberries and see if we can't design a better system. After all, this republic was founded by ordinary people taking the law into their own hands — they had to because most of the governor, judge and lawyer-types were quite comfortable in England, thank you. And don't forget that we have already agreed that the present legal structure doesn't work, so

---

* Not everyone believes that a rotten court system is a bad thing. David Hapgood in his interesting book, *The Average Man Fights Back*, reports the following statement by the Chinese Emperor K'ang Hsi: "...lawsuits would tend to increase to a frightening extent if people were not afraid of the tribunals and if they felt confident of always finding in them ready and perfect justice...I desire therefore that those who have recourse to the tribunals should be treated without pity and in such a manner that they shall be disgusted with law and tremble to appear before a magistrate."

we obviously have nothing to lose by making our own suggestions. Hey, leave a few raspberries for me, and why don't you jot down a few of your own ideas as we go along so that this becomes a two-way communication.

Before we get to specific suggestions for change, let's take a brief look around to see where we are starting from. As a society, we obviously have a fixation with trying to solve problems by suing one another. Nowhere in the world do people come close to being as litigious as we do. The result of this love of lawsuits, or perhaps its cause, — it's one of those chicken and egg problems — is the fact that, whenever we get into any sort of spat with anyone, or even think that we might get into one in the future, we run to a lawyer.* It's gotten so bad that people who suffer an injury have been known to call their lawyer before their doctor. But there is an odd paradox here. At the same time that we tolerate vast numbers of lawyers eating at the top end of our societal trough and are more and more likely to use them, public opinion polls tell us that our respect for lawyers has fallen so that we rate their trustworthiness below that of used car salespeople, undertakers and loan sharks. It's as if, the less we respect lawyers, the more we use them. Perhaps we're afraid that if we don't sue first, someone will get the jump on us. If you eat one more of those raspberries, I'll see you in court.

Have you ever thought about how people solved their disputes in other ages? Let's pretend for a moment that we are members of a society of deer hunters in an age when such things were still possible.** One fine fall morning we both set out bow in hand, you to the east and I to the west. Before long, you hit a high cliff and turn north. My way is blocked by a swift river, and I too turn north. My way is blocked by a swift river, and I too turn north. Without our realizing it, our paths converge. Suddenly, a great stag jumps from the underbrush and we both pull back our bows and let fly. Our arrows pierce the deer's heart from opposite sides, seemingly at the same instant.

For a moment we stand frozen, each surprised by the presence of the other. Than we realize what has happened and that we have a problem. To whom does the deer belong? We carry the

---

* There are close to half a million lawyers in the United States. New York City alone has more than 40,000. The New York Times reported that by 1977 many lawyers were charging $25 for each six minutes of their time. In San Francisco during working hours, one out of every three hundred people is a lawyer.

** Anthropologists will, I hope, accept this little fable as just that.

deer back to the village, each unwilling to surrender our claim to the other. After the deer is gutted and hung, we go to speak to the chief of our group who convenes a council of elders to meet late in the afternoon. Each of us has his say as to what happened. The deer carcass is examined. Anyone else who has knowledge of our dispute is invited to speak. Tribal customs (laws) are consulted, our credibility is weighed, and a decision is made — in time for dinner.

Now, let's ask ourselves what would happen today, if you and I simultaneously shot a deer (instead of each other) on the first day of hunting season and were unable to agree to whom it belonged. Assuming we didn't fight it out on the spot, but wanted the dispute resolved by "proper" legal procedures, lawyers would have to be consulted, court papers filed and responded to, a court appearance scheduled, words spoken in legalese, and a formal court decision written and issued. All of this for a deer that would have long since rotted away unless it had been put in cold storage. If the deer had been frozen, the storage costs would have to be added to court costs and attorney fees which all together would surely add up to a lot more than the value of the deer. Oh well, next time we had better go hunting at McDonald's where everything is delivered safely wrapped in plastic.

Seriously, what were the differences between the ways that the two societies resolved the problem of who owned the deer? The so-called primitive one did a better job, but why? Obviously because their solution was in proportion to the problem, while today we make the solution process so cumbersome and expensive that it dwarfs most disputes. The hunting society handled the disagreement quickly, cheaply and, most importantly, with a process that allowed the disputing parties to participate in and understand what was going on.* Simple, you say. Why then can't our dispute resolution procedure achieve even one of these goals? In large measure, because lawyers have vested financial and psychic interests in the present cumbersome way of doing things and have neither the motivation nor the perspective to make changes.

But isn't my view a bit radical? Isn't there something uniquely valuable about the great sweep of the common law down through

* In a criminal case (if one hunter had attacked and injured the other) you would also want to think about restitution (making whole) to the injured person and perhaps to his dependents.

the ages? Doesn't the majestic black-robed judge sitting on his throne mumbling esoteric nonsense somehow guarantee that God is in heaven, the republic safe, and that "justice will be done?" Not necessarily. History is arbitrary — our dispute resolution mechanisms could have developed in a number of ways. If our present system worked well, imposing it on the future would make sense. As, in fact, it hardly works at all, continuing it is silly. Those who get quite misty-eyed recounting the history, traditions and time-tested forms behind our present ways of doing things are almost always people that benefit by their continuance. Consider, too, that in North American we have no pure legal tradition, having borrowed large hunks of our jurisprudence from England, Spain, France, Holland, Germany as well as various Native American cultures.

OK, granted that there have been legal systems that worked better than ours, and granted that at least some change is overdue, what should we do? One significant reform would be to expand Small Claims Court. Like the system followed by the deer hunters, but unlike the vast majority of our legal system, Small Claims Court is simple, fast, cheap and allows for the direct participation of the disputing parties. Never mind that up to now Small Claims has been tolerated as a way to keep lawyers' offices clear of penny ante people with penny ante disputes. It's there, it works, and we can expand it to play a meaningful role in our lives.

As you know by now, Small Claims Court as it is presently set up has several disadvantages. First, the amount that can be sued for is ridiculously low. Second, the court only has the power to make judgments that can be satisfied by the payment of money damages. Third, many kinds of cases, such as divorces, adoptions, etc., aren't permitted. Why not start our effort to improve things by doing away with these disadvantages? Let's raise the maximum amount that can be sued for to $10,000.[*] I would like to suggest $20,000, but perhaps we should take one step at a time to limit attorney oppositon. An increase to $10,000 would be a significant reform — allowing tens of thousands of disputes to be removed from our formal legal system. One logical reason to pick $10,000 is that people can't afford lawyers to handle disputes for

---

[*] While most states limit Small Claims jurisdiction to $750 (California) or $1,000 (New York), there are exceptions. For example, the United States Tax Court has a very successful Small Claims procedure which allows claims up to $5,000.

amounts below this.* To illustrate, let's take a situation where Randy the carpenter agrees to do $20,000 worth of rehabilitation to Al's home. When the work is completed, an argument develops about whether the work was done properly according to the agreement. Al pays Randy $15,000, leaving $5,000 in dispute. Randy goes to his lawyer, and Al to his. Each has several preliminary conferences after which the lawyers exchange several letters and telephone calls. Eventually, a lawsuit is filed and answered, a court date is obtained many months in the future and then changed several times, and, finally, a two-hour trial is held. Randy's lawyer bills him $1,255 (25 hours x $50 per hour) and Al'a charges $960 (24 hours x $40 per hour), for a total fee of $2,215. The dispute takes eleven months to be decided. In the end, Randy is awarded $4,500 of the $5,000.

This is a typical case with a typical solution. Between them , the lawyers collected almost half of the amount in dispute and took most of a year to arrive at a solution that very likely left both Randy and Al frustrated. Don't you think that Randy and Al would have preferred presenting their case in Small Claims Court where it would have been heard and decided in a month? Of course, either of them could have done worse arguing the case himself, but remember, when the legal fees are taken into consideration, the loser would have had to do a lot worse before he was out-of-pocket any money. Randy recovered $3,500 with a lawyer, but after subtracting the $1,255 lawyer fee, his net gain was only $2,245. Al ended up paying $4,460 ($3,500 for the judgment and $960 for his attorney). Thus, if a Small Claims Court judge had awarded Randy any amount from $2,246 to $4,459, both men would have done better than they did with lawyers. Of course, if this sort of case were permitted in Small Claims Court, there would be two big losers. Can it be a coincidence that lawyers (through their control of every state legislature) make sure that Small Claims maximums are kept as low as possible?

---

* I believe that there are persuasive reasons for limiting the role of lawyers in addition to the fact that they cost too much. Such a limitation would require fundamental changes in our adversary system and is the subject for a broader book. For a good history of how our adversary system evolved from barbaric practices such as trial by battle, how it all too often serves to obscure rather than expose the truth, and how it protects the interests of the already strong and powerful (those who can afford a good mouthpiece) at the expense of everyone else, see *Injustice For All*, Strick, Putnam, $8.95.

The second great barrier to bringing cases in Small Claims Court is the fact that, with a minor exception, the court is limited to making money judgments. Think back for a moment to our problems with the twice-shot deer. How does the award of money make sense in this situation? In our Small Claims Court, the Indian who didn't end up with the carcass would have had to sue the other for the fair market value of the deer. What non-sense — if we are going to have a dispute resolution procedure, why not permit a broad range of solutions such as the deer being cut in half, or the deer going to one hunter and six ducks going to the other in compensation, or maybe even the deer going to the person who needed it most. Using an example more common at the end of the 20th century, why not allow a Small Claims Court judge to order an apartment be cleaned, a garage repainted, or a car properly fixed, instead of simply telling one person to pay X dollars to the other. One advantage of this sort of flexibility is that more judgments would be meaningful. Under our present system, tens of thousands of judgments can't be collected because the loser has no obvious source of income. We need to get away from the notion that people who are broke have neither rights nor responsibilities. All people need both.

Lawyers and judges often contend that it would be impossible to enforce judgments granted under a more flexible approach. Perhaps some would be hard to keep track of. Certainly it might require some experimentation to find out what types of judgments will work and which will not; however, since it is often impossible to collect a judgment under the present system, it can't hurt to try some alternatives.

The third big change that I propose, and the one that would truly make over our court system, involves expanding the types of cases that can be heard in Small Claims. Why not be brave and take the 20 most common legal problems and adopt simplified procedures enabling all of them to be handled by the people themselves without lawyers? Why not open up our courthouses to the average person, who after all, pays the bills?

To accomplish this democratization of our dispute resolution procedures, I suggest dividing Small Claims Court into several separate divisions, each one responsible for a broad area of common concern. For example, there would be a landlord-tenant and a domestic relations.* Each division would have the authority to consider a broad range of problems and solutions falling within its area of concern. Today, if you have a claim against your landlord (or he against you) for money damages, you can use Small Claims only if the claim is for $750 or less. If you want a roof fixed, a tenant evicted, or to protect your privacy, etc., Small Claims Court can't help you.** The Canadian province of British Columbia has already put all landlord-tenant disputes in what amounts to a Small Claims format, easily and cheaply available to both landlord and tenant. Why can't we?

A domestic relations Small Claims Court could include simplified procedures to help people handle their own uncontested divorces, adoptions, name changes, guardianships, etc. safely and cheaply. And why not? Even with considerable hostility from lawyers and court personnel, over 20% of the divorces in California are already handled without a lawyer. When I suggest that people should be encouraged to handle their own domestic problems in a Small Claims type forum, I'm not advocating sensible safeguards be dropped. For example, if a divorce involves children, you would want to have someone trained in the field carefully examine the parents' plans for custody, visitation and support to see that they are reasonable.

Without going into detail, I suggest that if we took lawyers out of our domestic relations courts, we would save not only millions of dollars and hours, but more importantly, we would lighten the heavy burden of hostility and anxiety that the parties must now bear. Our present system, in which parents and children become clients to a "hired gun" (the lawyer) is a bad one. By definition, the client role is weak and the gun fighter role strong. This imbalance commonly results in lawyers making critical decisions, affecting the client's lives, sometimes obviously, sometimes subtly. All too often these decisions benefit the lawyer and his bank balance to the detriment of both the client's psyche and pocketbook. The lawyer, after all, is paid more to fight, or at least to pretend to fight, than to compromise. I have seen dozens of situations where lawyers have played on people's worst instincts

* There is nothing new about the idea of dividing a court by subject matter. This is already done in our formal trial courts and works well.
** As I pointed out in Chapter 20, some evictions can be brought in Small Claims if a number of conditions are met, but it is commonly unwise to do so.

(paranoia, greed, ego, one-upmanship) to fan nasty, little disagreements into flaming battles. Perhaps mercifully, the battles normally last only as long as the lawyers' bills are paid.*

I could list a number of other areas of law that could be converted to a Small Claims approach (auto accidents, simple probates, perhaps even some criminal cases), but I am sure you get the point. We must take control of the decision making processes that affect our lives. We must make ourselves welcome in our own courts and legislatures. We must stop looking at ourselves as clients and start taking responsibility for our own legal decisions.

Let's assume now that no matter what the obstacles, we are going to expand drastically the role of Small Claims Court. In the process of so doing, we will need to make a number of changes in the way the court now operates. It will be a good opportunity to throw out a number of existing procedures that owe more to history, than to common sense. Here are a few ideas:

1. Before people present their dispute for resolution as part of a court proceeding, they should be encouraged to talk it over among themselves. This seems to be basic common sense, but a face-to-face meeting to find out if a compromise is possible isn't part of the present system. A meeting with someone who has training as a mediator could occur at the courthouse or, perhaps, at a less intimidating location in the community, as a regular part of every case.

2. Let's make our court one of truly easy access. This means holding weekend and evening sessions. This is being done now experimentally in a few areas, but should be routinely available everywhere. When court is held at 9 a.m. on weekdays, it often costs more in lost job time for all the principals and witnesses to show up than the case is worth.

3. Let's get the judge out of his black robe and off of his throne. There is a part of all of us that loves the drama involved in seeing our magistrate sitting on high like the king of England, but I am convinced by my own brief experience as a "pro tem" judge that this is counter productive. We would have a lot less confrontation, and a lot more willingness to compromise if we got rid of some of the drama.

---

* In an interesting article entitled "Valuable Deficiencies, A Service Economy Needs People In Need", in the Fall 1977 Co-Evolution Quarterly, John McKnight points out that "The Latin root of the word 'client' is a verb which translates 'to hear', 'to obey'."

4. While we're making changes, let's make a big one — let's throw out the adversary system.* It contributes a great deal to posturing and obfuscation and little to arriving at a dispute resolution process that everyone can live with. We must move toward systems of mediation and arbitration in which, instead of a traditional judge, we have someone whose role is to facilitate the parties arriving at their own solution — deciding it for them only if they arrive at a hopeless impasse. Big business, big labor, and increasingly even lawyers are coming to realize that arbitration and mediation are good ways to solve problems.** What I have in mind is something like this: All the parties to the dispute would sit down at a table with the Small Claims employee (let's drop the word "judge"). This person would be trained for the job, but would not normally be a lawyer. The court employee would help the parties search for areas of agreement and possible compromise and then help them define any areas still in dispute.***

5. Appeal rules should also be changed. The present California system which allows only the defendant to appeal to Superior Court and allows lawyers on appeal is nuts. All too often corporate defendants who have lawyers on retainer use the present system to frustrate consumers who have won in Small Claims Court. It is my belief that no appeals should be allowed in Small Claims Court — the amounts in question just aren't worth it. If appeals are allowed, lawyers should be prohibited.

I don't mean to suggest that the changes I propose in this short chapter are the only ones necessary. If we are going to put the majority of our routine legal work in Small Claims, it will require turning our dispute resolution process on its head. Legal information must be stored and decoded so that it is available to the average person. Clerk's offices, and the other support systems

---

* Roscoe Pound, distinguished legal scholar, said it better than I can, "The doctrine of contentious procedure...is peculiar to Anglo-American law...(it) disfigures our judicial administration at every point...(it) gives to the whole community a false notion of the purpose and end of law...Thus, the courts...are made agents or abettors of lawlessness." This quote is reported by Anne Strick in *Injustice For All*.

** California has adopted a procedure which even allows cases that have been filed in court to be diverted to an arbitration procedure.

*** The best source of information about mediation as well as a number of other approaches to getting non-lawyers involved in their legal system is *The People's Law Review*, Warner, Addison-Wesley Publishing Co. This book gathers people's law ideas from all over the country and is the most exciting book I have worked on. See the back of this book for more information.

surrounding our courts must be expanded and geared to serve the non-lawyer. Legal forms must be translated from "legalese" into English. Computer systems must be developed to bring legal information into our living rooms.

Let's illustrate how things might change by looking at a case I recently saw argued in a northern California Small Claims Court. One party to the dispute (let's call her Sally) arranged fishing charters for business and club groups. The other (let's call him Ben) owned several fishing boats. Sally often hired Ben's boats for her charters. Their relationship was of long standing and had been profitable to both. However, as the fishing charter business grew, both Sally and Ben began to enlarge their operations. Sally got a boat or two of her own and Ben began getting into the charter booking business. Eventually they stepped on one another's toes and their friendly relationship was replaced by tension and arguments. One day a blow-up occurred over some inconsequential detail, phones were slammed down and Sally and Ben each swore never to do business with the other again.

Before the day of the final fight, Sally had organized two charters on Ben's boat. These were to have taken place a week after the phones were slammed down. For reasons unconnected with the argument, the charters were cancelled by the clubs that had organized them. Ben had about a week's notice of cancellation. He also had $600 in deposits that Sally had paid him. He refused to refund the deposits. Sally sued him in Small Claims Court for $700 ($600 for the charter fee and $100 for general inconvenience).*

Testimony in court made it clear that charters were commonly cancelled and were often replaced by others booked at the last minute. Ben and Sally had signed a "Standard Marine Charter Agreement" because it was required by the Coast Guard, although they had never in the past paid attention to its terms. They had always worked out sensible adjustments on a situation-by-situation basis, depending on whether substitute charters were available and whether the club or business cancelling had paid money up front, etc.

When Ben and Sally first presented their arguments about the

---

* As we learned earlier, Sally can't recover for inconvenience, so her maximum recovery would be $600.

$700, it seemed that they were not too far apart as to what would be a fair compromise. Unfortunately, the adversary nature of the court system encouraged each to overstate his (her) case and to dredge up all sorts of irrelevant side issues. "What about the times you overloaded my boat?" Ben demanded. "How about those holidays when you price gouged me?" Sally replied. As the arguments went back and forth, each person got angrier and angrier and was less and less able to listen to the other.

The result was that after an hour of testimony the judge was left with a confused mish-mash of custom, habit, maritime charter contracts, promises made or not made, past performance, etc. No decision that he arrived at was likely to be accepted by both Ben and Sally as being fair. Indeed, unless he gave one or the other everything he or she requested, both of them would surely feel cheated. That is not to say that the hearing was all bad — some good things did occur. The dispute was presented quickly, cheaply and each person got to have his or her say and blow off some steam. All of these things would have been impossible in our formal court system. However, if Small Claims Court could be changed along the lines suggested above, a better result might have been reached.

Suppose that instead of a formal courtroom approach Ben and Sally are first encouraged to sit down and talk the dispute out. If this fails, then the next step is to sit down in a non-courtroom setting with a court employee who is trained as a mediator and whose purpose is to help Ben and Sally arrive at a fair compromise — a compromise which might provide a foundation for Ben and Sally to continue to work together in the future. Only if compromise is impossible, would there be recourse to more formal proceedings.* I am convinced that Ben and Sally would have worked out a compromise at the first or second stage.

One final point. Today lawyers are still trying to plug the holes in the rotten dike of our present legal system. Tomorrow the dike will burst and many of our present ways of doing things will be washed into the history books. Small Claims Court will survive the deluge and will expand. The danger is that lawyers will try to control Small Claims Court so that their attitudes and prejudices

---

* If we put domestic cases into Small Claims Court (and even if we don't), it is essential that we work out a non-adversary way of handling them so that bitterness and bad feelings are kept to a minimum instead of inflated as is now the case.

dominate it as they have dominated every other mechanism our society has to resolve disputes. To allow this to happen is to destroy much of the value of expanding Small Claims Courts. And don't minimize the danger. As I have noted, under a so-called "consumer reform" approach, lawyers are already serving in the role of advisor in several California judicial districts and you can expect an effort to have it institutionalized soon. It is all too likely that under the guise of trying to protect us from ourselves, an effort will also be made to have everyone see a lawyer as part of the Small Claims procedure. Remember, it is our lawyer-dominated state legislature that makes Small Claims rules and our lawyer-dominated Judicial Council that carries them out.

Have I rambled for a long time? I guess I have. But now it's your turn. If you have any ideas and comments on how you would like to see Small Claims Court changed or expanded, let me know care of Nolo Press, 950 Parker St., Berkeley, California 94710.

Ralph is the leader of the "do your own law" movement on the West Coast. As a co-founder of Nolo Press and the author of numerous books and articles aimed at giving the non-lawyer so-called "legal information" to deal with their own life decisions, he has constantly tried to expand the areas in which people can help themselves.

Ralph has a license to practice law. He doesn't use it. Instead he gives lectures and workshops on such subjects as "Tenant's Rights", "Law for Unmarried Couples", "How To Use Small Claims Court", "Debt Problems", etc. to groups all over California. As part of doing research for this book, Ralph has served as a Small Claims Court judge (pro tem) in Berkeley, California.

Ralph lives in Berkeley. He likes dogs, cats, hanging out in the woods, pretty ladies, the full moon and Japanese food.

Nolo Press consists of a group of people (some lawyers, some not) who came to see much of what passes for the practice of law as being mumbo jumbo and paper shuffling designed by lawyers to mystify and confuse. Just as the majestic black-robed judge is in reality only a lawyer wrapped in a black shroud, sitting on a wooden platform at the end of a drafty room, a lawyer is all too often a fellow who turns up mumbling esoteric nonsense when ordinary folks take their wallets out.

Started in 1971 with *How To Do Your Own Divorce,* Nolo Press has become a positive energy force for people who want to open up our legal system and make its so-called trade secrets available to all. Nolo has now published close to a dozen books aimed at providing people with the information necessary to help themselves. In the process, it has helped the authors to maintain their own self respect in a field where bank balances have often been more prominent than ethics.

Our books have been written, illustrated, designed and printed by a group of friends headquartered in Berkeley and Occidental, California. Without ever planning to, we have created our own cottage industry. We hope you get as much out of reading this book as we did in making it, and we would be delighted to get any feedback you would care to send our way.

NOLO PRESS
SELF-HELP LAW SERIES

Nolo Press publishes a comprehensive series of self-help law books designed to help you untangle the mumbo jumbo and obfuscation that often surround even the simplest of legal procedures. With these books, you are able to take care of many common legal situations, from forming a small corporation to getting a divorce or planning your estate. With attorney's fees running at an inflated $40-$150 an hour, our self-help law series offers a sensible and financially sound alternative. It also provides a means of taking a more active role in the legal matters that affect you.

THE PEOPLE'S LAW REVIEW
An Access Catalog To Law Without Lawyers
Edited by Ralph Warner $8.95

This book is about eliminating the need for lawyers. It gathers resources and ideas that point to ways in which access to everyday law and the resolution of common disputes can be opened to all. Included are materials on doing away with the adversary system, mediation, the possibilities of expanding small claims court, law in China and Cuba as well as nuts and bolts sections that supply practical information on all sorts of legal areas from getting a book copyrighted to handling your legal research.

> "A Whole Earth Catalog of law"
> Time Magazine
> December 8, 1980

Business & Finance

BANKRUPTCY: DO-IT-YOURSELF:

By attorney Janice Kosel. Shows exactly how to file for bankruptcy in California. Comes complete with sample forms and
worksheets to compute property and debts, and a complete set of
forms which you can tear out and use. Discussion on whether or
not bankruptcy makes sense as a solution to your financial problems, when to file, what property you can keep in bankruptcy,
and much more. $12.00

BILLPAYERS' RIGHTS

Fourth Edition. A constructive guide for those who find themselves over their heads in legal debts. Contains information
on wage and bank account attachments, car repossession, child
support debts, student loans, bankruptcy, etc. Also, detailed
information on how to deal with collection agencies, including
sample letters and agreements. Recommended by the Washington
Post, L.A. Times, S.F. Examiner, Berkeley Co-op News and S.F.
Action. $6.95

HOW TO FORM YOUR OWN CALIFORNIA CORPORATION:

Third Edition. This extremely popular book, by California attorney Anthony Mancuso, includes tear-out Articles, Bylaws,
minutes and stock certificates and all the instructions necessary to set up your own small California corporation. The tax
consequences of incorporating are thoroughly discussed. Takes
advantage of the 1977 Corporation law. For profit corporations
only. $15.00

PROTECT YOUR HOME WITH A DECLARATION OF HOME-
STEAD:

Fourth Edition. Your house can be protected from your creditors
up to $40,000 under California law only if you file a homestead.
Here we tell you how to do it cheaply, easily and legally. An
invaluable gift for the new homeowner. Includes recent law
changes. Also contains information and forms on exemptions for
mobile homes and houseboats. $5.95

SMALL TIME OPERATOR:

How to start your own small business, keep your books, pay your
taxes and stay out of trouble. Includes a year's supply of ledgers and worksheets. This book is for people who have an idea,
a skill or a trade, and the desire to make their living working
for themselves. By Bernard Kamoroff, C.P.A. Distributed by
Nolo Press. $7.95

220

CALIFORNIA NON-PROFIT CORPORATION HANDBOOK:

Second Edition. Completely revised to cover all the new law changes. Step-by-step instructions on how to choose a name, draft Articles and Bylaws, attain favorable tax status, and get your non-profit corporation started. Thorough information on federal tax exemptions which groups outside of California will find particularly useful. $15.00

Wills & Estate Planning

PLANNING YOUR ESTATE WITH WILLS, PROBATE, TRUSTS & TAXES:

By attorney Denis Clifford. This comprehensive book contains a great deal of legal information about the practical aspects of death. Here in one place for the first time, Californians can get information on making their own will, alternatives to probate, planning to limit inheritance and estate taxes, living trusts, and providing for children. A person's right to die and legal rights to a funeral of his or her own choice are also discussed in detail. This book will greatly increase the information the average person has about estate planning. $15.00

Family & Friends

AFTER THE DIVORCE:

HOW TO CHANGE CUSTODY, SUPPORT AND VISITATION ORDERS: By attorney Joseph L. Matthews. Picks up where How To Do Your Own Divorce leaves off. A concise guide --- with all legal forms and instructions --- explaining how child support can be changed. Also contains new joint custody rules with necessary forms to make custody changes. $12.00

THE PEOPLE'S GUIDE TO CALIFORNIA MARRIAGE & DIVORCE LAW:

By attorneys Ralph Warner and Toni Ihara. Contains invaluable information on community and separate property, names, debts, children, buying a house, etc. Includes sample marriage contracts, a simple will, probate avoidance information and an explanation of gifts and inheritance taxes. $7.95

HOW TO DO YOUR OWN DIVORCE IN CALIFORNIA:

This famous book revolutionized the divorce field by making it clear and simple to the layperson. Tells you the practical things you need to think about and gives information and advice on making your various decisions. Shows exactly how to do your own. Over 200,000 copies in print have saved Californians more than $15 million in attorney fees. New edition includes 1979 law changes. (California only) $8.95

A LEGAL GUIDE TO LESBIAN/GAY RIGHTS:

By attorneys Hayden Curry and Denis Clifford. Discusses in detail such areas as raising children (custody, support, living with a lover), buying property together, wills, etc. Comes complete with sample agreements. This is a national book, produced by Nolo Press and published by Addison-Wesley. $10.95

HOW TO ADOPT YOUR STEPCHILD:

By Frank Zagone. This straightforward guide shows you how to prepare all the legal forms necessary to adopt your stepchild in California. Includes information on how to get the consent of the natural parent and how to conduct an "abandonment" proceeding if necessary. Private and agency adoptions are not covered. $10.00

MEN'S RIGHTS:

By attorney William Wishard. Discusses rights and issues with which men (and women) are concerned: living together, abortion, fatherhood, employment, child custody, support and visitation, and much more. Distributed by Nolo Press. $6.95

Rules & Tools

CALIFORNIA TENANTS' HANDBOOK

Sixth Edition. Sound practical advice on getting deposits back, breaking a lease, getting repairs made, using Small Claims Court, dealing with the obnoxious landlord and forming a tenants' union. Contains numerous sample letters and agreements as well as a Fair-to-Tenants tear-out lease and rental agreement. "...sharper than a serpent's tooth." --- Herb Caen, S.F. Chronicle (over 80,000 in print) $7.95

HOW TO CHANGE YOUR NAME

California Edition. Second Edition. Changing your name is cheap and easy. This book comes complete with all the forms you need to do it yourself. Full information on women's name problems with special attention to women who want to retain, or return to, their own name after marriage or divorce. This book is primarily valuable to Californians. $7.95

DON'T SIT IN THE DRAFT:

By Charles Johnson. A draft counselling guide with information on how the system works, classifications, deferment, exemptions, medical standards, appeals, and alternatives. $6.95

IMMIGRATING TO THE U.S.A.:

This is the best, moderately-priced guide for non-lawyers who are interested in immigration. Written by an experienced immigration lawyer who himself immigrated to the U.S., it discusses student visas, preference categories, marrying a U.S. citizen, work permits, non-immigrant visas, deportation and much more. Immigration forms are reproduced along with instructions on how to fill them out. $7.95

LANDLORDING:

A practical guide for the conscientious landlord and landlady. Covers repairs, maintenance, getting good tenants, how to avoid evictions, record keeping and taxes. "A step-by-step guide to acquisition of business sense." -- San Diego Tribune. This is a large book, 8½ x 11, 253 pages, produced by Express Press and distributed by Nolo. $15.00

RIGHTS OF THE ELDERLY & RETIRED:

Attorney William Wishard has written the first excellent treatment of legal and practical problems that affect the elderly. Included is information on social security, medicine, nursing homes, housing problems and solutions, debt problems, taxes and much more. Anyone who is retired or cares for or loves an older person, will benefit from reading this book. Distributed by Nolo Press. $6.95

MUSICIAN'S GUIDE TO COPYRIGHT:

By Erickson. In just 85 pages, this book does exactly what its title says. It is highly informative and answers most of the important questions a musician will have regarding her/his work. Distributed by Nolo Press. $5.95

ORDER FORM

Quantity	Title	Price	Total
_____	How to Adopt Your Stepchild	10.00	
_____	After the Divorce	12.00	
_____	Bankruptcy: Do-it-Yourself	12.00	
_____	Billpayers' Rights	6.95	
_____	How to Form Your Own California Corporation	15.00	
_____	How to Do Your Own Divorce in California	8.95	
_____	Planning Your Estate	15.00	
_____	*A Legal Guide to Lesbian/Gay Rights	10.95	
_____	Protect Your Home with a Declaration of Homestead	5.95	
_____	*Immigrating to the U.S.A.	7.95	
_____	*Landlording	15.00	
_____	California Marriage & Divorce Law	7.95	
_____	How to Change Your Name	7.95	
_____	California Non-Profit Corporation Handbook	15.00	
_____	*The People's Law Review	8.95	
_____	*Rights of the Elderly & Retired	6.95	
_____	Everybody's Guide to Small Claims Court	7.95	
_____	*Small Time Operator--Managing Small Businesses	7.95	
_____	California Tenants' Handbook	7.95	
_____	*Men's Rights	6.95	
_____	*Musician's Guide to Copyright	5.95	
_____	*Don't Sit in the Draft	6.95	

*Applicable in all 50 states

1st Subtotal	_____
20% DISCOUNT	_____
2nd Subtotal	_____
tax (see below)	_____
postage (see below)	_____
TOTAL	_____

Name _____

Address _____

City _____

State, Zip _____

For postage and handling please enclose 85¢ for the first book and 35¢ for each additional book. California residents include tax (6½% BART & Santa Clara county, 6% elsewhere).